M000315172

The Mystery of Sophia

ALSO BY ROBERT POWELL AND ESTELLE ISAACSON

Gautama Buddha's Successor:
A Force for Good in Our Time (2013)

THE MYSTERY OF
SOPHIA

BEARER OF THE NEW CULTURE
THE ROSE OF THE WORLD

ROBERT POWELL
ESTELLE ISAACSON

Lindisfarne Books

2014

2014
LINDISFARNE BOOKS
AN IMPRINT OF STEINERBOOKS/ANTHROPOSOPHIC PRESS, INC.
610 Main St., Great Barrington, MA 01230
www.steinerbooks.org

Copyright © 2014 by Robert Powell and Estelle Isaacson.
All rights reserved. No part of this publication may be
reproduced, stored in a retrieval system, or transmitted, in
any form or by any means, electronic, mechanical,
photocopying, recording, or otherwise, without the
prior written permission of the publisher.

Cover image: *Sophia* by Estelle Issacson
Design by William Jens Jensen

LIBRARY OF CONGRESS CONTROL NUMBER: 2014943354

ISBN: 978-1-58420-175-5 (paperback)
ISBN: 978-1-58420-176-2 (eBook)

CONTENTS

Acknowledgments

The authors of this book express their heartfelt gratitude to Karen Rivers for her inspiring foreword and to Claudia McLaren Lainson for her dedicated support and helpful suggestions with regard to the text of this book—and with heartfelt thanks also to Richard Bloedon for shepherding this book right from the beginning and for his skilled editorial assistance.

An immense debt of gratitude is owed to numerous sources—see appendix—for transmitting invaluable ancient wisdom and for pioneering new knowledge in our time relating to Sophia.

We would also like to thank publisher Gene Gollogly of SteinerBooks for taking on the manuscript and enabling this book to become available, and William Jens Jensen for his meticulous work in making it possible for this book to appear in print.

There are many others who have helped in one way or another to whom our gratitude and appreciation are extended, without naming everyone explicitly.

Robert Powell and Estelle Isaacson
March 25, 2014
Festival of the Annunciation
of the Archangel Gabriel to Mary

In the beginning was Sophia,
and Sophia was with God, united with the Logos.
Sophia was in the beginning with God.
All things were made by the Logos and Sophia,
and nothing that was made
was made without the Logos and Sophia.
Sophia is Wisdom,
And Wisdom is the Light of creation,
And the Light shines in the heavens,
And the Angels radiate it forth.

FOREWORD

Karen Rivers

This book brings together the mystical revelations of Estelle Isaacson, a contemporary mystic and seer, with the research of Robert Powell, an internationally read author whose background combines Sophiology and Astronomy. This collaborative work pioneers a prescient interrelationship of the mystical and scholarly, the experiential and the interpretive, bringing to the fore a multi-faceted perspective about the presence of Sophia at this time in the unfolding of human evolution.

From diverse, yet complementary perspectives, both Estelle Isaacson and Robert Powell address the topics of the increasing presence of Sophia through Her descent toward the aura of the Earth, and the ever-increasing activity of the Holy Soul fructifying spiritual communities with the activation of spiritual love and inspiration. Estelle Isaacson reveals the intimate presence of Sophia through her mystical experiences wherein she perceives Sophia proclaim decisive directives for humanity, urgent pleas to awaken to the spiritual reality of creation, and Sophia's effulgent outpouring of love for every living being. Robert Powell brings to light a gradual descent of Sophia from the heights of spiritual reality toward the atmosphere of the Earth. His research incorporates the descriptions of Sophia at various stages of approach to the Earth, making reference to the writings of Dante Alighieri, Vladimir Soloviev, Madame Blavatsky, Rudolf Steiner and the Russian mystic, Daniel Andreev, all of whom experienced Sophia in spiritual revelation.

Sophia permeates the ground of existence. She is the spiritual essence within all matter. She embodies the wisdom of creation, and bears the presence of the Divine into human souls and communities as the agent of spiritual love and inspiration. She inspires human souls through the Holy Soul, who is the holiness of the creation, interweaving between God and humanity. The creative force of the Holy Soul awakens the impulse to unite in spiritual community through the love that weaves between spiritually striving human beings. Sri Aurobindo portrays the Holy Soul in the following passage from his epic work, *Savitri*.

> The silent Soul of all the world was there:
> A Being lived, a Presence and a Power,
> A single Person who was herself and all
> And cherished Nature's sweet and dangerous throbs
> Transfigured into beats divine and pure.
> One who could love without return for love...
> She rocked the cradle of the cosmic Child
> And stilled all weeping with her hand of joy;
> She led things evil toward their secret good,
> She turned racked falsehood into happy truth;
> Her power was to reveal divinity.
> Infinite, coeval with the mind of God,
> She bore within herself a seed, a flame,
> A seed from which the Eternal is new-born,
> A flame that cancels death in mortal things.
> The intimacy of God was everywhere,
> No veil was felt, no brute barrier inert,
> Distance could not divide, Time could not change.
> A fire of passion burned in spirit-depths,
> A constant touch of sweetness linked all hearts,
> An inner happiness abode in all,
> A sense of universal harmonies,
> A measureless secure eternity
> Of truth and beauty and good and joy made one.
> Here was the welling core of finite life;
> A formless spirit became the soul of form.
> —Aurobindo, *Savitri* (book 2, canto 14, "The World-Soul")

Sri Aurobindo poetically captures the essence of the Holy Soul, portraying Her as a mediating and unifying agent of the multiplicity of living creatures. She is the agent that draws us to God, and to one another in spiritual love. We seek Her that God might dwell in us.

When Sophia lives in our soul, Her forces work within us to bring to realization truth, beauty, and goodness, for, in the words of Thomas Merton:

> Sophia is the mercy of God in us. She is the tenderness with which the infinitely mysterious power of pardon turns the darkness of our sins into the light of grace. She is the inexhaustible fountain of kindness, and would almost seem to be, in herself, all mercy. So she does in us a greater work than that of Creation: the work of new being in grace, the work of pardon, the work of transformation from brightness to brightness *tamquam a Domini Spiritu*. She is in us the yielding and tender counterpart of the power, justice and creative dynamism of the Father. (*Hagia Sophia*, 1963)

Historically, the focus of human worship has metamorphosed from matriarchal devotion to the Earth Mother in ancient and indigenous cultures, to patriarchal devotion to the Transcendental Father in Western civilization. Consciousness of the Divine Feminine has been forgotten for the most part during the past three thousand years. Now, as Sophia is reemerging in human consciousness, we have a new task before us. As the domain of the Divine Feminine awakens higher *soul forces*, the realm of the Divine Masculine addresses higher *spirit forces*. The higher soul forces that work through the Beings of the Divine Feminine have been left unheralded during patriarchal dominance. The challenges of our time call for an integration of the higher soul forces and the higher spiritual forces within us.

Thus we have now entered a Sophianic millennium wherein the presence of a potent spiritual force is being revealed to human consciousness in a new way. The mysteries of the Divine Feminine can be penetrated through the study of theology, world religions, ancient mythology, and now also through science, unveiling the glory and wisdom of creation. A path toward a future relationship with the Divine Feminine has been laid that has the potential to integrate and include theology, science, religion, devotion, and service. It is possible to enter into a new stage of evolution where human consciousness comes to honor every aspect of creation, the immanent and the transcendent simultaneously through wisdom and love.

Through the mystical visions of Estelle Isaacson you will enter a realm of blessedness, a rarified atmosphere of luminosity and mystery that touches a sequestered reservoir in the depths of the human soul. Her intimate experiences with Sophia open a portal for everyone to enter into a personal relationship with Sophia. In the second part of this book Robert Powell addresses Sophia and world evolution. He guides us through the stages of Sophia's descent toward the Earth through the lens of astronomy. He introduces the Sophianic Trinity and the Rose of the World, a vision of a future humanity living in consciousness of Sophia's guiding light.

As Sophia's presence becomes more prominent at this time in human evolution, the question arises: How is humanity to evolve into a new, mature, holistic relationship with the Feminine Face of God and simultaneously cultivate spiritual balance with the Masculine Face of God that will work through the human intellect, through the heart, and into human deeds that will reflect a conscience of stewardship for Mother Earth and the kingdoms of Nature and the attainment of peace in human relationships? The collaboration of Estelle Isaacson and Robert Powell brings forth realities of a spiritual unfolding that centralize Sophia as the guiding inspiration for the future. The mystical visions and spiritual research in this book grace the reader with a love and wisdom that flow from the heart of Sophia, Herself.

Karen Rivers, Ph.D.
Director of the New Chartres Academy
Co-founder of the Sophia Foundation

PREFACE

Robert Powell

WHO IS SOPHIA?

Who is Sophia, and what does the coming Age of Sophia signify for humanity and for the Earth? From the Bible it is known that *Sophia* is the Greek word for "wisdom." In the Old Testament this word is expressed in the Hebrew as *Hokmah* (pronounced "Chokmah" with a guttural "ch"), meaning *wisdom*. When the Old Testament was translated into Greek, the word *Hokmah* was translated as "Sophia." In the English translation of the Bible, this is translated as "wisdom." If one reads the Book of Proverbs, one finds there words that Sophia speaks through King Solomon. It has been said that Solomon was regarded as the wisest human being of antiquity. So great was his fame on account of his wisdom that people came from all over the ancient world to seek him out, including the fabled Queen of Sheba. She came from afar to drink from the wisdom of Solomon. Solomon was a human being who had a special relationship with Sophia, Divine Wisdom. Various books of the Old Testament are attributed to Solomon, including the Book of Proverbs. All of these books speak of Sophia. These are called the Wisdom Books of the Old Testament.[1]

If we read the Book of Proverbs, we see words that Sophia speaks in the first person. This answers one of the questions that are often raised with regard to Sophia: Is divine wisdom simply

---

1   Schipflinger, *Sophia-Maria.*

an attribute of God? We speak of God's power, God's wisdom, and God's love. But, if you read the Wisdom Books in the Old Testament, it is clear that it is not simply an attribute of God but an actual being, because She speaks in the first person. She says, for example: "I was present at the beginning of the creation...participating at the side of the Lord in the work of creation" (Prov. 8:22, 30). This statement tells us something about Sophia. It is a matter of an actual being, whose nature is wisdom, and who participated in the work of creation. It is clear also from the words spoken that Sophia is a feminine being—a great, divine feminine being.

In the following chapters, Estelle Isaacson's visions reveal the omnipresence of Sophia and Her love for every aspect of creation in both the heights and the depths. The Divine nature of Sophia can be heard in the words through which Estelle shares her visions. It is an unimaginable gift to us all that these visions have come into the world. Through Estelle, Sophia speaks to each and every one of us.

Part One

Estelle Isaacson

Fourteen Sophia Visions

SOPHIA!

You of the whirling wings,
circling, encompassing energy of God:
you quicken the world in your clasp.
One wing soars in heaven,
one wing sweeps the earth,
and the third flies all around us.
Praise to Sophia!
Let all the earth praise her!

—HILDEGARD OF BINGEN

I

The Second Coming of Christ
and the Descent of Sophia

In the beginning of the vision[1] I saw a ray of beautiful blue-violet light. I entered into the light and saw a sphere moving toward me. I felt enveloped by the love and peace of the Divine Mother. Soon I came to realize that I was experiencing this love through the essence of the individuality of John the Baptist. The living energy of Shambhala was within his being as a stream of radiant blue light that was constantly flowing through and raying out to the world. I experienced the silence of Divine Love at the very core of his spirit. I beheld the stars of his being and could see the power of creation that is in him—*the seed forces*. I entered into the "world that he is," where everything was imbued with blue-violet light, and silence pervaded the atmosphere.

In mystical communion with him, I received the following vision and message:

This is the time of the second coming of Christ. And the second coming of Christ is announced from Shambhala, which has been issuing forth this great announcement for almost a century. The beings that serve the Mother bear this message from the mineral kingdom to the plant kingdom, the animal kingdom, and humankind—to all who can hear the news: that He comes again in clouds of glory! He is here! His body is the

---

1   This vision occurred on December 9, 2011.

3

Earth. His breath is the wind. He is holding the Earth in His loving embrace.

Shambhala is awakening. Beings that have had to hold their silence may now speak and act. There is a great stirring and awakening in Shambhala. Shambhala has been in a time of winter, as it were, a time of holding in, a time of withdrawal. But because more human beings are awakening to the Divine Mother, the beings at the center of the Earth are stirring and are beginning to rise up and prepare for the descent of Holy Sophia—the Heavenly Daughter; and Christ is preparing the way for Her in his second coming.

His *first coming* was to prepare hearts to attune to the Father. His *second coming* is to prepare hearts to receive Sophia. He will bring Mother and Daughter together on Earth, thereby reuniting the Earth Mother and the Divine Daughter.

A great awakening is on the horizon for humanity as Sophia draws ever nearer to the spiritual sphere of the Sun. And through our Sun, She will ray out to the world a *new sustaining life force*. This is a life force that has been present in this world mostly within a very small number of mystics, prophets, and seers who have been able to find Sophia in the heavens; they have embodied this life force energy and rayed it out to others. With the descent of Sophia and Her entrance into the Sun sphere, this life force energy will ray out to the whole world. A great healing will occur; just as mystics ray out healing, so shall Sophia emanate healing to the *entire world*—even through the rays of the Sun.[2]

There will be twelve spiritually awakened females incarnated on Earth at that time. (I saw this happening a few hundred years from now.) They will reside at certain places in the Earth, and not in close proximity to one another. They constitute a council of

---

2   This is clearly a reference to the "woman clothed with the Sun" in Rev. 12:1—"Behold a great sign appears in heaven: a woman clothed with the Sun, with the Moon under her feet, and on her head a crown of twelve stars." For a discussion of the stages of Sophia's descent, see chapter 16 of this book.

the female counterparts to the twelve bodhisattvas. These twelve will embody Sophia in a sense—their hearts will be vessels for Holy Sophia. The twelve communities wherein each resides will receive Sophia's grace and love through these women. And these communities will be bastions of peace wherein the veil is very thin between the worlds. These twelve individuals will be dwelling fully in their resurrection bodies, for they each shall have been raised from the dead. They will be in resurrection bodies like unto Christ's risen body. And Christ and Sophia will dwell together, united, as their center. They will be keepers of Dharma.

As Sophia's time of descent draws ever nearer, Her angels will be set free for a season when they will be free to minister to humankind. They will do Sophia's bidding on the Earth.

Now, in the present time, they are somewhat bound, for in some respect the Divine Feminine is still bound.

The Divine Mother can be unbound for specific individuals who are willing to descend—to find Her and break Lucifer's chains that bind Her. There are individuals who shall do this. They shall lift Her veil and behold Her; thus shall the work of Her salvation go forth.

This work began when Christ descended into the center of the Earth after His death on the Cross. And it was there that He beheld the Mother. He descended with the memory of Her glory— the glory that She had from the beginning of creation. He went through the depths of hell to find Her. And there She was, having been cast down into the center of the Earth, hidden and cloaked in all the deepest, darkest layers of evil, which were so frightening that only a pure soul could penetrate through.

It was the spirit of John the Baptist who was able to accompany Lazarus's soul to the center of the Earth.[3] They could both

---

3   Reference to the chapter in *Through the Eyes of Mary Magdalene* where this is discussed: Isaacson, *Through the Eyes of Mary Magdalene: A Trilogy* (vols. 1 and 2). Volumes 1 and 2 of this trilogy were published in 2012, and the third volume is expected to appear in 2014.

descend to Her, but could not yet free Her. Only Christ could do this. Lazarus and John the Baptist were witnesses of the Mother in Her state of captivity. She was able to teach them many things. But they had not the power to loosen the cords that bind Her.

For Christ, it was necessary that some prepared human souls witness the state of the Mother in the darkness of the underworld. Lazarus was able to recollect these things after he returned to Christ Jesus and brought this witness to Him. Christ knew where He would go at the time of His death. He knew that He would go to the Mother. This began His work of salvation for Her.

At the time of His second coming, He inspires human beings to turn their hearts to the Mother. In so doing, human beings are able to free Her for their own selves—which will eventually lead to Her being free for all, so that She may attain the glory that is rightfully Hers.

All of you who are beloved of Christ (for you who are initiated in the mysteries of Christ's deeds on Golgotha are called "beloved"), are being asked by Sophia's angels and the beings who serve the Earth Mother to arise and awaken to the calling to invoke the divine spiritual world and pray for the Mother—to seek to know Her love and to bring this love to others.

When John the Baptist was incarnated, a magnificent bird would appear, sent by the Holy Soul[4] working together with the Holy Spirit. He was told that he was to start a community—a community in the wilderness that would be prepared to receive the Messiah. And now the individuality of John the Baptist is united with the Holy Soul to inspire *spiritual communities*— communities of hearts—to usher in the second coming of Christ. Whereas previously the communities were physical and gathered in the wilderness, now they are gathering in spirit. And whereas

---

4   For a discussion of the significance of the Holy Soul, see chapter 17 of this book.

the Messiah first incarnated in a human body, now He comes in spirit and shall manifest to spiritual communities.

O Beloved, do not fear what is coming. There must be darkness so that the light may manifest more fully. The light is always there. It has always been there.

The bitter cup[5] is coming once again. There is a second Gethsemane for Christ-bearers. There is a second betrayal for Christ-bearers. Do not turn away from the bitter cup. It is by accepting the bitter cup that you shall enter into the sweetness of Holy Sophia's love and grace. You shall know a greater love; this love will be the sweetest nectar to your soul. And you shall be strengthened so that you may be able to accept what is coming.

Remember, when your head seems to be engulfed in dark thoughts that are not your own, to behold your feet. For His Word is the lamp to your feet. You know that the serpent has the power to bruise you at your heel. But you, through the power of the Word and the light of Christ, have the power to crush the serpent's head. Remember that even though your head may be in darkness, envision your feet in the light; and in that light, you have the power to walk through the fires. Remember that even though your head may tell you that you will be burned when you walk through fire, your feet know otherwise.

As the light grows in you, you will face many trials. Remember that with God all things are possible—*all* things. There is truly nothing to fear. The trials will be for but a moment. Let yourself walk in Christ. Let His feet be your feet—His feet that walked on water, for the water upheld His body.

Your work is to do what your heart tells you to do. Follow your heart's yearnings.

Attune yourself every day to your spiritual community, that you may be strengthened by the grace that flows from heart to

---

5   This is a reference to Christ's deeds in Gethsemane and to the "bitter cup" in Matthew 26:42.

heart. Put yourself at the center of your community and receive love from your community and give them your love. It takes only a moment to connect. This is very powerful, for it is truly sacred magic.

O Beloved, look up and feel the love coming to you on the rays of the Sun.

O Beloved, the Eternal One is beholding you now and shall hold you forever in His gaze. He considers you, each and every one, and holds you in your suffering. Offer your suffering to Him, and you shall be purified and you shall be healed.

O Beloved, all is well.

Amen.

*She is the Force that leads
across the ocean of the world of change (samsara).
She is the Holy Wisdom of all that exists.*

—Brahma Vavarta Purana, 21

2

THE ANGEL OF FREEDOM

I was above the Earth and saw the Angel of Liberty, the angel of freedom. She was weeping for the Earth.

She gave to me the following message[1]:

If human beings truly desire freedom, they must awaken and be able to behold how they are in bondage. I can do nothing for human beings who refuse to do anything for themselves in gaining true freedom.

I inspire freedom, and I am *always* inspiring freedom. The inspirations of the Evil One, who is anti-freedom, are now enveloping the Earth. Pray vigilantly that human beings may awaken to true freedom—to think the thoughts, speak the words, and perform the acts that can lead to true freedom.

Even just one individual who is able to overcome the mind programs and will think the thoughts of freedom—freedom-inspired thoughts—can effectuate mighty change. It begins with one person, and then flows to other souls. Through this can there be a peaceful inner resolution, a wave of mighty force that can prevail over the dark forces.

Holy Sophia is coming. She will shine through the darkness, and touch the hearts of those who are able to remain free. She will come in Her glory, in Her resplendent beauty, with all Her wisdom and Her unchanging, everlasting purity. Christ, in the etheric body of the Earth, shall bring Her here as a great blessing for all the Earth.

After the travails, the wars, and the destruction, She will be the light breaking through the clouds, touching all those

---

1   This vision was given on January 18, 2013.

who have found the Christ in their hearts—those who rise triumphant, who heed not the terrible temptations to cast down the Christ.

There will be temptations to believe that there is no God, no Godhead, no Christ, no Savior for this world. Many will succumb. Because of this they will become easy prey for the Evil One and his forces. They will fall into apathy, and shall have little care for another life, neither will they care for their own lives. Like sheep they will follow the Dark Master, even as he leads them over the cliff, while the Christ-bearers must hold in Silence the truth.

All you bearers of the Christ, heed these words. The light in you is enough. Your light is needed in this world. Your light is the power to change the whole world.

Believe in Him who is the Lover of your soul. Keep His face ever before you. Believe in His power. He watches over you in the night. He teaches your soul all things that you should know. The light in you is His Light.

As you let this flame live in your heart you will become the vessel for Christ to work His mighty miracles.

The Archangelic Being of John

I then saw the being of John the Baptist. Again, he was most radiant, and appeared as a brilliant Host, the Holy Spirit streaming from him in the form of a Dove. A message was given to me (and to all) through him:

O daughter, do you hear the harmonies of the coming glory—the glory of Holy Sophia? I herald Her Coming!

As Her light breaks forth from the wide expanse of the cosmos, I announce She is coming! Her world is a world of peace and freedom.

She offers Herself as our new world. She is the Holy City, and She is descending toward the Earth.

It is possible to know Her, and to enter into Her peace, and Her rest, even during tumult.

O beautiful child, you are Her seedling. She is the life force coursing through you. She is the life-giving sap of the Tree of Life, and the Tree of Life is within you.

I then spoke this prayer to Holy Sophia: *May Thou guide and protect all who seek for Thee. May all hearts consecrated to Thee remain pure, and undefiled. May they withstand the temptation to give up, to turn away, to grow cold!*

The message continued:

O Child of Light, think of your precious heart as being the abode of the Holy Queen of Heaven. You are Her guardian. You are Her knight. You must stand at the gates of Her City, and allow only those who are benevolent and pure to pass through the gates.

You are a peaceful knight. As a guardian you are able to discern the darkness, and see it, and name it. You do not succumb to fear or anger. You do not go out to do battle, but you protect the inner sanctum of your heart so that Wisdom may reign there forever.

The individuality of John the Baptist is like unto an archangel—a great folk spirit. He is the *original human being,* and is rich beyond measure in human experience! He has lived many, many lives.

More than any other human being he understands how to truly be human. He is the leader of human evolution, the prophet, the guide. In his archangelic state he is able to guide any human being on the path of evolution—he can guide the individual while he also guides universal evolution.

He freely gives guidance to all who ask in purity. He prepares souls to become Christ-bearers. He is the bearer of the Holy Spirit.

I was in mystical union with him! So full of ineffable love was I, merging in the light with him! My soul expanded out, and I was reflecting his light.

Then a terrible demon came bounding out of the dark void toward our Light. But as it grew near, gnashing its teeth and charging like a bull, it suddenly became completely docile, tamed; and it retreated—its head bowed, body softening. It could not prevail over the immense Love pouring forth from the being of John.

Then, in vision, I beheld John the Baptist when he was dwelling in the wilderness before Jesus came to him for baptism. He was dressed in a hide, carrying a walking stick. He had been in the wilderness for many years. I saw how he was attacked many times by demons. But no matter what came against him—whether taunting, mischievous elementals, or the most maleficent sub-earthly demons—he could not be deterred from his path. He would acknowledge them with but a glance—but it was a *glance of love!*—and then continue on his way. It was as if a rabid dog were charging at him, but then once the dog gets close, it feels so much love that it instantly becomes tame. Then the dog becomes his friend. This is what happened with the demons. There was no fear in him, only Love.

And this is what happened when I merged with his light! We became like shining Hosts in the middle of this great fury, all this darkness. When the dragon came I had no fear at all! I felt the very same love that I feel when a heavenly being is approaching me. Thus the demon was transformed in this incredible love, and can now become a servant of the Good.

This is the way to transform the dark side, the evil forces. This individuality can show us how. He is ever present for the world. He is present like the saints are present, but with even greater power because he is such an advanced human soul! He is *the* answer, and we, united with him, are the answer to the question of how the good can prevail.

We who have the light within can love the evil until it is transformed. He will show us how to find that love within us—the love that transforms all darkness. He embodies the *whole of human experience*, and ensouls the potential for every human being. Thus he can lead us to our greatest potential, which is Love.

We came here because of Love. We remain for Love. We shall return for Love. Love is the highest principle of the Universe. We can find this Love on Earth even while we behold its antithesis— the deepest, darkest of all evils.

Indeed, as we behold the darkness we find the Love that we are. The darkness is transformed. There is no greater power than Love.

The dark forces gain power through inducing suffering, torture, trauma, and unimaginable atrocities. They generate fear, despondency, and hopelessness. People will believe that they are feeling their own feelings, when in actuality they are feeling the projected vibrations coming at them. If, however, we can refrain from falling into the trap of these *generated* emotions, then we shall be victorious.

We can say no to this! We can find the Love, even in the darkest hours. We can feel love for all, holding in consciousness the original intention that the human race came to fulfill in its earthly probation—in the realization that humanity is beautiful and good, and that all human beings have the flicker of light of goodness and beauty within!

We can hold to Christ's original promise that His redemption is for *all*—both the good and the evil. We can behold how He loves every human being, and remember that this life is only a tiny point in time within the eternities. We can remember who we truly are, and remember the other as well.

When we feel weak we can call upon saints and angels to assist us in reclaiming the Love. This is the greatest work: to hold in Love everything and everyone.

Perfect Love casteth out fear.

Amen.

Love is the way messengers from the mystery tell us things.
Love is the mother.
We are her children.
She shines inside us,
visible-invisible as we trust or lose trust,
or feel it start to grow
again.

—RUMI

3

THE CHILD-SELF OF THE WORLD SOUL

As the vision began,[1] I was in a spiritual garden full of beautiful, hovering flowers in unearthly colors. Beyond this garden a sphere of white light beckoned to me, and I deepened into it until all I could see was white light. The truly sacred space of this sphere was pervaded by silence.

I became aware of enormous beings holding the sphere in place, so to speak. The loving face of Christ appeared, radiating glorious light as He beheld me. He directed my gaze to the Earth. I was afraid to look because of what I might see. I found I could keep my eyes on His eyes while at the same time beholding the Earth. Great darkness covered the Earth, causing the Earth to appear misshapen. Immense suffering arose in my soul!

Because I was able to look at the Earth through His eyes, the fears then melted away.

I saw how the Earth is overrun with technology—with electrical grids all but covering the planet. These grids, and the overuse of technology by individuals, can easily cut people off from the angelic sphere—and this is especially so when the people do not acknowledge or believe in the angels. Through the greater use of technology there is the possibility of becoming ever more mired in illusion and trapped in the material world.

Then I was moving toward the Earth, and a message from Christ opened to me from a golden book He held in His hands:

---

1   November 9, 2012.

Behold the Earth and all that She is. Behold Her travail and all that She suffers. There is indeed a darkness that attempts to cover the Earth, even to consume the Earth and possess it. It wants to inspire the hearts of human beings to turn against each other, to inspire war and hate. But it cannot and will not take hold of every human heart, for there are hearts that have been prepared to receive Me. Those who receive Me become beacons of light shining through the darkness, and this light has the power to call forth the angels.

I have said that the Kingdom of God belongs to the little child, and indeed you must become like little children to pass through these times. Every little child is surrounded by angels; and so shall you be comforted and strengthened if your faith is like unto a child's. Be close to the children. Work with the children. The same angels that protect them shall protect you also. Find your light heart in the children and let go of your heavy heart.

The health and future of the planet depends upon the health and well-being of the children. When children are surrounded by heavy-hearted adults, their hearts can also become heavy. They can become adults prematurely. Create spiritual community with children at the center, keeping the children as a focus. Then the community is encircled by angels—the angels of the children. It will become more and more challenging for human beings to reach the angelic sphere, although the scripture is true that states: "...and a little child shall lead them."

There is a little child within you—your own child-self. And this child shall lead you, and the children around you shall lead you.

Strengthen and support any endeavor that works to care for children and do this out of love, not fear. Think of the needs of the children—their basic physical and spiritual needs. Think of your own child-self's needs and work to fulfill those needs. The angels will assist you and inspire you.

I then saw the little Christ Child! I saw Him as the World Child, the *Child-Self of the World Soul!* And He lives! The Christ Child is ever-present. He is a part of the World Soul and His angels are countless and eternal.

Behold the Christ Child!

Through the simple act of beholding Him with faith, you shall find yourself surrounded by angels.

Behold how He rests in his Mother's arms and does not fret or worry. He is at rest. The Christ Child sees only the goodness and the beauty in every one. By His simple act of beholding the goodness in all, goodness and beauty are able to shine through.

Little children also have this innate gift of beholding the Good. They trust. They have hope and compassion as a natural way of being.

Speak with the angels of the children. If you offer yourself in service to them, they can work through you on behalf of the children. The Christ Child is within every little child. It is the Christ Child who leads us to the Mother's heart where we are comforted and protected, and filled with love.

The Christ Child is ever so sweet! I was able to hold Him in my arms. He was so very beautiful, glowing with golden light and loving me and allowing me to love Him! When I am with the Christ Child I don't have to have answers, or figure everything out, or solve every problem. Those are the plagues of the adult mind. The grown-up mind thinks it has to figure everything out.

All is well; all are being watched over; we are free to *be*. With Him, we can let the heaviness go and choose to feel the love and incredible peace that is all around Him.

It is by love and through love that we will know where to go and what to do. The children will teach us, they will show us how to be present—how to live in love. When you are with little children, you know that they naturally live in present time.

It is very important that we refrain from imposing our fears onto the future world. Be as a little child who lives in the now and beholds the goodness and the beauty that is ever-present in everyone.

Even though it may seem that the Earth is covered in darkness, and the health of the world is failing, there is still hope.

There is hope in the Christ Child of the World Soul. Those who can find Him will be able to receive His youth forces, in which there is utter peace and also great sacred power—the power to create. The little child is Heaven on Earth. Find the little child within your own self, and the little child within everyone. Serve and comfort that little child.

And find the Christ Child within the World Soul, wherein you will know the power of transformation. If your own child-self is hurting, help her to find healing. Let the child-self play and rest, and find comfort in the Mother's arms. The Divine Mother shall not turn away from her little children. Her arms are open and She receives them!

Help the children to know their Divine Mother through story and play, and through emulating the Divine Mother. The children of the world are crying for their Divine Mother—longing to know Her. The power of transformation is indeed great when the children of the Earth are reunited with their Divine Mother; for the power of regeneration is within this reunion. There is growth and abundance, as well as joy and peace. A child who has found the Mother and feels Her embrace has the power to transform many lives. Let us do all we can to bring the consciousness of the Divine Mother, and Her love, to the children and to the child that is within every human being.

I saw the angels that serve the Divine Mother and Holy Sophia—so powerful and love-filled are they! In their presence it is not possible to feel fear.

Go to the Mother in prayer, and let Her hold you. Rest your head against Her heart and let Her love you. Take all your troubles and worries to Her and give them to Her. She will gaze upon you and tell you that you are the most perfect and beautiful child She has ever seen. She will weep tears of joy when you have come to Her, because She loves you so much. She is waiting for you to come. She will not judge you for being so sad or for being so angry. She will listen and wipe your tears away. Look at Her beautiful face—how Her eyes never want to leave yours! She would gaze upon you for all eternity because She loves you infinitely.

Your soul needs nothing more than what She can give to you. Her love is sustenance for your soul.

When you were spiritually created and gestating in the Cosmic Womb, the Divine Mother received a part of you into Her being and this part of you became a part of Her. Thus She carries you in Her Being. You are ever-connected to Her by the very fact that the seed of your being lies eternally in Her. She feels your pain but She also feels the promise and the hope that you are to all of creation.

And this happens in part with earthly mothers.

Mothers, while pregnant, receive in a mysterious way some of the DNA of the fetus. The DNA of the fetus continues to live on in the Mother, and this can cause challenges for the mother, both physically and emotionally; but it can also strengthen and empower the mother.

Science is beginning to discover the truth of this—that there is some sharing of DNA that happens in a *reverse* way—in that the child shares its DNA with the mother.[2] This is an earthly representation of what happens between the Divine Mother and all of Her spiritual creation. We all dwell within Her Great Being, and because of this we are truly One in Her.

Do not think of others as being so separate from yourself. If you can feel that you are a part of the whole, you will be a great healer. If you can feel the same way gazing upon someone who seems dark and evil as you feel when you behold someone who seems light and beautiful, then you are becoming like the Mother who loves all of Her children the same, and does not choose one over

---

2   This is known as "microchimerism"; here is a relevant link: www.sciencedaily.com/releases/2008/05/080502134332.htm.

the other. In this way you become a great healer. You bring others into that state of wholeness. You return the child to its mother's arms. When this happens, the transformation is profound.

And each person is a microcosm of the whole—a microcosm of the Earth. When one finds healing for one's heart, it truly changes the Earth.

On the Cross of the World Body
The World Soul reveals Herself:

Living in five radiant streams
Through Wisdom,
Love,
Power of Will,
Sense of the All,
And sense of the "I,"

The Spirit of the World
Is realized
In Her.

—RUDOLF STEINER

4

Sophia Bearing the Cross of the World

As the vision opened,[1] I immediately was gazing upon the Earth from the spiritual realm. My focus was being drawn to the darkness on the face of the Earth, where there were so many very dark places that looked almost like black holes. There were also other places where, instead, beams of light shone from the Earth, penetrating space. I felt tremendous grief over the darkness that I beheld. Then, turning my gaze toward the beams of light, I was drawn into a particular one, where I experienced the light that emanates when one enters into the Mystery of Golgotha, witnessing the deeds of Christ. Within my own soul I experienced the sharp duality in the Earth—the contrasts of light and darkness.

For several nights prior to this vision, I had been experiencing Sophia as if Her body were wrapped around the Earth, the Earth being within Her womb; and the Earth was quaking, almost convulsing in pain. She was holding it and containing its pain, which I wished with all my heart I could assuage. She was grieving over the Earth; I strove with Her as She agonized.

It was then as if the Earth became a Cross and She was kneeling beneath it; I mourned with Sophia, sorrowing for what has been, for what is, and for what will be done in the Earth. Sophia knows what the Earth will eventually become; this was ever present in Her also, alongside the grief.

---

1   November 5, 2010.

I was taken to the Cross, where I saw Mary Magdalene; I experienced Christ and Sophia within Magdalene—*the Divine Male-Female principle united in her to witness the sacrifice of the Son.*

I was then drawn into a previous point in time, wherein Mary Magdalene was initiated in the union of Christ and Sophia. As I entered into this moment, I did not know if my human body could contain the experience. I found that it was mostly unspeakable!

THE UNION OF CHRIST AND SOPHIA

Mary Magdalene bore the union of Christ and Sophia beneath the Cross. She was "pregnant" with their union, we could say. And although she was suffering exceedingly, and wanted to die with Him, she could not *die,* because of what was then *living* in her. With the power of the life of Christ and Sophia within her, she was humbled in her humanity, so aware of the "finiteness" of being human, while at the same time she was a vessel for the Divine, feeling the merging of the Divine in her.

What I experienced next, I experienced not only as a past event in the biography of Mary Magdalene, but I also was *given* the same experience. I am not sure of the extent of Magdalene's conscious experience. Therefore, I will relate what happened in my own words, as I experienced it.

I rose up from the Cross and was taken into the "world that I am"[2] where I found myself to be in a spirit-garden of luminous, hovering flowers in unearthly colors. I was then allowed to experience what happened to Magdalene on the third day of her initiations in the cave.

Out on the horizon of the world-that-I-am, in the rosy-golden atmosphere of light, I saw two spheres of brilliant light appear,

---

2   The author has experienced the soul as a "world unto its own self." All souls may be experienced this way—every soul in its various stages of development, as some souls are more developed than others. See Teresa of Avila's *Interior Castle* for further explanation on this topic.

which drew nearer to me. The spheres of light were Christ and Sophia—my soul instantly recognized them. As they approached, my entire being seemed to open to them as if I were a blossom opening to the sun in salutation. Before the incredulous eyes of my soul, they merged together and became one great sphere of light; this caused my entire soul to be in ecstasy, flooding my soul with light. The sphere of their union then merged with me until I was fully one with them in brilliant light. This is what I had also experienced in the vision of the third day of Mary Magdalene's initiations (found in Book II of *Through the Eyes of Mary Magdalene*); this time I was experiencing it from another perspective, and my understanding was increased.

I then saw a mystical child descend out of the union of Christ and Sophia into my third eye chakra—the child entered into me and descended into my heart, which became like a womb. From the child in my heart there emanated the seven mothers of humanity; they were the mothers of the seven root races. I was in awe as they stood before me, each emanating the seven colors of the rainbow. Each of their compassionate faces were a different color and were uniquely beautiful. The seven mothers returned to me the seed that was "destroyed" by Lucifer. To briefly explain: before I began incarnating in this world, Lucifer had destroyed my "sphere" and my "seed." I cannot define everything about this "seed," except to say that the "seed" was my power to increase—the "holy grail," as it were. In an earthly sense, the seed could be seen as the promise of spiritual posterity; but there is a greater spiritual aspect to this principle that I find very hard to define. This seed was returned by the mothers; I understood that this "returning of the seed" would happen over time.

I saw all humanity pass before me in the "world that I am," emanating out from the seven mothers; I loved all of humanity. The mothers surrounded me as I stood in the center; angels gathered around us in concentric circles. We then became the *seed of life*—I saw the seven rings of the seed of life! I experienced the seed of life as a *living* spiritual form.[3] It was with all of this—the seed of life and all contained within it—that Mary Magdalene was "pregnant" as she knelt beneath the Cross: pregnant with the unity of the community of humanity. It was as if she had all of humanity inside of her, under the Cross.

From her perspective, I looked up at Christ on the Cross; never had I seen Him looking so beautiful on the Cross—He became like a rainbow pouring out streams of colors. The seven mothers were all around the Cross, each one of them a witness and a vessel of their people's suffering and transgressions; He took this in and held it within His Being. He bore suffering and darkness from past, present, and future, absorbing it all into the blissful rainbow light of His Being—their colors merging with the colors of His Being. This rainbow light then poured out upon me. I cried, "Why do I deserve this beauty and this grace—to behold Him like this?"

He took all of this into His Being—everything from the seven epochs of time, from every stage of evolution. This brought Him so much pain! He knows every soul; He beholds every soul; He feels the pain of every soul. I was with Him in His beholding of all of humanity. He held all the pain and darkness in His eternal compassion.

His compassion! The honeyed nectar that sweetens the bitter pain! He freely pours His compassion out in His tears, like the dew that falls from Heaven to cool our passionate fires—the living water that quenches the thirst of our desolate souls, which have become so dry as we wander in the wilderness of this world.

He freely gives of Himself to any soul who seeks for Him.

When we enter His suffering, He baptizes us with His tears; and the tears of our suffering merge into the ocean of His tears.

Our blood becomes the space in which He can dwell.

---

3   Isaacson, *Through the Eyes of Mary Magdalene*, book 2, appendix 5, offers further description.

We become light to the world—a light unto the world that nourishes the spiritual beings. Our prayers become the answer to the prayers of the angels. And we become the living prayers of the angels as we gather together in His name, in communities dedicated to Christ and to Sophia, who then are wedded within us. Our true creative power is thereby restored to us, and we may create sacred places in the Earth—places of truth, beauty, and goodness. We can begin to create these places now, as seeds for the future.

I saw a great temple erected to Christ and Sophia in the spiritual world. It emanates pure white light; its outer courts are Silence, and within is the Holy of Holies, wherein dwells the Word. And the Word shall be born from the Silence. I saw that the Word shall come forth from the Holy of Holies and shall go forth to nourish the people. Its power shall surround the Earth, borne by the Holy Spirit to communities that are being prepared through the Holy Soul to receive these blessings. Such communities will experience a Pentecost that will take place after purification that comes through suffering—a purification by fire—so that they shall be ready to receive Him into their midst. This shall be a work of holy suffering, for it shall sanctify and prepare the ground to be fertile, so that when the seed of life is planted therein it will be able to take root and flourish. These are the places where Heaven and Earth will come together. And Christ shall be ever present in the suffering.

You are stewards with Sophia over the Earth, to hold Her in Her quaking, in Her grief. You can bring Her through this challenging time, holding Her in prayer and being with Her in Her laboring. Prepare to receive Her. Pray for all the beings that serve Her on this Earth.

Have courage to be a part of a spiritual community, for this is the answer to so many problems in the world. Think of those places on the Earth where there is not true spiritual community and become that for them. Do it for the Congo. Do it for Zimbabwe. Do it for Haiti, for the Mid-East, and for other places. This is Sophia's request. She is calling out to Her children who are seeking for Her, the ones who know Her—which are few. If you would know Her, if you would truly serve Her, then draw yourselves together in love on the behalf of those who cannot. No longer be an island to your own self. Yes, you are all very much alone; you are "hermits" in one way or another. But allow your hearts to join together in spirit as a unity in order to heal this world, in order to generate the consciousness of spiritual community. As you do this, the angels of Sophia will help you in direct ways. They will inspire you and bring to you the resources you need. You cannot know how great the effects are of this communal work She gives to you. There is great power in your gatherings and in your intentions.

And the peace of Christ and Sophia shall be with you even in your tribulation.

Amen.

I am the beauty running through the world,
to make it associate in ordered groups—
the ideal held up before the world to make it ascend.
I am the Eternal Feminine.
I was the bond that held together the foundations of the
universe...
I extend my being into the soul of the world...
I am the magnetic force of the universal presence and the
ceaseless ripple of its smile.
I open the door to the whole heart of creation:
I, the Gateway of the Earth, the Initiation...
In me, the soul is at work to sublimate the body—Grace to
divinize the soul.

—TEILHARD DE CHARDIN

5

SOPHIA'S PRESENCE IN THE TRANSFIGURATION AND AT GOLGOTHA

As the vision began,[1] I found myself enveloped in soft rosy-hued and lavender light, feeling the deepest sense of peace. The presence of my friend's yet unborn baby was with me. Above was a ring of pulsing soft white light. I was caught up in wings of light and taken through the opening. I was in a state of tremendous love, feeling myself expanding out. This was so familiar to my soul. As I passed through the ring of light I then entered into an incomprehensible state of being—which I find very challenging to put into words. I somehow went into a dimension that seemed so much further than I usually go.

I was then in the presence of Sophia, in Her Silence. *O Holy, Holy Sophia!*

I was overcome by the love that I felt—the unconditional Mother-love as I rested in the cradle of stars in the sphere of Sophia. The stars above metamorphosed into Sophia's visage, becoming Her face as She gazed upon me. Her face was blooming like a cosmic white rose, the petals opening to receive me.

The star above my head moved gently down through my being, coming to rest in my heart—which then became like a reflecting pool, mirroring Sophia's starry light in the star of my own heart!

In the Silence She beheld me, and beheld Herself within me; and my soul opened to receive Her. From the depths of my soul

---

1   October 29, 2010.

arose a wish—one that had whispered in the depths for a very long time. And now this came forth from my soul: I wanted to receive Her completely...and I asked that this may be.

Her response was immediate, withholding nothing. From Her breast outpoured the divine milk of Her Grace, bathing my entire soul. From Her Heart poured the sweet honey of Her Love. In this act of purification of heart and soul, She utterly gave Herself to me. The milk and honey penetrated me fully, and nourished my soul. I was astounded to receive such a bequest!

After this, She spoke, Her words resonating throughout my entire being, Her voice like soft, tinkling chimes:

> I give the Milk of Divine Grace and the Honey of Eternal Love to all those who seek My face. I bless you with My Grace and the sweetness of My Love. I hold you to My breast and nurture you with My Love.
>
> I have heard your entreaties; you have cried out to be held by your Mother; and I have heard your cries through ages and lifetimes. How I have ached to hold you and to bring you out from the desolate places in which you have been wandering; for I have watched you wander in the fallen world amongst thorns and thistles!

Sophia's words then flowed out toward the Christ, and she continued—addressing the Christ:

> Oh My Son! I beheld Your sacrifice. I watched You leave Your high place and descend to the fallen world. I felt Your pain—how painful it was to be a human being! I saw you quake and shudder as you descended from the realm of Light down to the briar patch of darkness! Oh My Son, I watched You walk amongst the children of humankind who would treat You with scorn, who hated You! They took Your name in vain, cast You down! I saw their hearts harden against You and felt the pain it caused—how Your heart shook within Your breast because of the great love You felt, which went unreceived! Oh My Son! How beautiful to see you stretch forth Your hand

to heal so many of their soul afflictions! And how marvelous that some came and their hearts were opened. They had faith in You and were healed; and their faith healed Your own heart's pain for a time.

Oh My Son! You knew human love. You felt human love! And on the wings of what was possible by and through human love, You were borne up and transfigured, to become a shining star for all humankind! The star-that-You-are had merged into Your human body; and I met you there in Your Transfiguration. In Your Transfiguration Your human body was transfused by the glory of the star that You are. In that moment Your earthly body became a heavenly body!

After these words, I went into a very long period of silence while witnessing the Transfiguration of Christ. I was present to behold His Transfiguration—but can scarcely write all that I witnessed. Sophia was in some way mysteriously involved with His Transfiguration. She was hovering above, with numerous saintly souls of prophets streaming toward Christ, while Moses and Elijah appeared on either side of Him, revealing themselves to Peter, James, and John. Christ Jesus was radiating fulsome light, such as is incomprehensible to our normal human eyes!

When I descended back toward my own being, I felt tremendous pain in my body, which was the commensurate pain of Christ in being human.

Sophia again spoke to Christ:

I beheld You in Your Transfiguration; and I came to You as Your consort and beheld You. You received My light into Your being; and I gazed upon that light, My light within Your Being. You took My light into Yourself and reflected it outward, that a part of Me would be borne by You through Your life as Christ Jesus—through Your passion. Our union, the heavenly-earthly union, was not made complete in Your Transfiguration, but You received My light into Your being, that My love could radiate from You to the humanity that I love. And My love went forth with You.

I am the rose who overcomes the thorn.

I then found myself in the Mystery of Golgotha, beneath the Cross, where the Blessed Mother and Mary Magdalene were ministering in silent prayer. Sophia was present through both of them—so that She was present to witness the Passion of Christ through the one who was pure, and through the one who was fallen. These two individuals represent the two aspects of our own souls: the original, chaste soul, and the fallen aspect.

Indeed, a part of the Divine Feminine went through the Fall (like Mary Magdalene) while another aspect of Her remained in the original, pure form (like the Virgin Mary). *The former aspect descended to the Earth, and dwells in Shambhala, while the latter remained in the starry realm.* And it is Christ who returns the fallen to a glorious state, for He redeems the fallen. He restores the Divine Feminine to Her rightful place. Christ loves the fallen; and He goes out after Her to restore Her. He calls Her to the bridal chamber.

The Divine Mother has not the desire to cast off the earthly. She does not pine to be rescued; She does not desire to turn away from the Earth. She has willingly sacrificed Herself for the Earth and all of humanity, remaining hidden in the depths. This is so in order to allow the world to be a place of opposition; for, by Her descending into the depths, the Earth was then able to harden and densify to such an extent that humanity would also densify. This then becomes the perfect place for evolution to occur. All human beings must work to remember their divine origins while forces of opposition act upon them. Human beings must experience suffering, toil and death until they awaken and rise up and remember their divine nature.

Sophia continued:

Christ is your bridegroom and He comes for you. He goes to the depths for you, and He guards you in your depths. He beholds the star that you are, which you have not been able to know in your depths.

Awake and arise! Go out and find Him, for He waits for you in the bridal chamber; and the door is open, and all that you are is holy to Him.

And you also shall be transfigured, that your soul may receive Sophia's light and love; and you shall become a beacon of light to others.

Through Sophia and the Holy Soul you shall go out and lighten the darkness of others, that they may also awaken and arise and see their darkness and say: "This is not I." Then shall they know their own I AM presence. And they shall be pierced with the I AM presence; and profound peace shall then be their discourse.

It is Sophia who brings the children of humanity to Christ, the great Healer, the great Redeemer. And Heaven and Earth can then come together in human hearts—through the union of Christ and Sophia within.

To achieve union with Christ: this is Sophia's gift and promise to humanity. Do not fear the opposition, for it is providing the way for you to evolve. It is what your soul needs at this time. After much tribulation comes the gift. Sophia is with you in your times of trial, watching over you.

And when the refining fires have done their work and you are born anew, she presents you to Christ as the gift.

He has bought you with His sacrifice. You are an extraordinary gift. And through your own sacrifices, you are able to meet Him in His sacrifice and you may then experience union with Him. This union shall bring about the new Heaven and the new Earth, which is the marriage of Christ and Sophia, which is eternal, having no end.

Amen.

Sophia is God's sharing of Himself with creatures.
His outpouring, and the Love by which He is given, and
known, held and loved.
She is in all things like the air receiving the sunlight.
In Her they prosper.
In Her they glorify God.
In Her they rejoice to reflect Him.
In Her they are united with Him.
She is the union between them.
She is the Love that unites them.
She is life as communion, life as thanksgiving, life as praise,
life as festival, life as glory.

—Thomas Merton

6

SOPHIA, HOLY BEGETTER OF THE GOOD

In vision I saw the holy women.[1] Together they radiated the colors of the rainbow. It was very healing to be in their presence as all of their colors emanated. The following message was given through them:

There is a need now to cultivate love and goodness wherever possible: to find the spark of true life, and draw that life forward; to bring life to light in the people with whom you associate, as well as in your gardens and in nature. Find the spark of light, the spark of life, and nurture it.

In every way that you cultivate life you are strengthening the life body of the Earth, and your own life body. Care for the body of the Earth and your own life body out of love.

The true life is being undermined, and even attacked, by the mechanical coldness of the Antichrist. The Antichrist is the taker of life, and uses the light of life for his selfish purposes. He wants to take that life into his own self to gain greater power.

Whereas the Antichrist *takes* life to add to his own life, the Christ *gives* life freely to all who follow Him. He is the source of life.

The spark of life within all is holy and sacred, for it is the light of Christ. When one is able to behold that light in others, one activates the seed that was planted in them by Christ: the seed of all potential, the seed of resurrection.

---

1   The following is a message given at Eastertide, March 30, 2013.

Those who awaken to the seed within themselves have the power to awaken others, and to heal others. There is great potential for goodness, for healing, for love to prevail over any dark force. Love is greater than any other force or power that is present on the Earth at this time.

There are certain individuals who are in the public focus as leaders of groups, countries, or religions. Surround them in prayer, that the spark of light within them can be strengthened in love, and that they can awaken and become free—so that those who follow them may also find freedom.

Ponder over who these individuals might be. Think of those who have the power to affect many lives. By way of example, the new Pope is the focus now of billions of people. He has the power to affect many. Surround him in mighty prayer.

He stands as the earthly head of Christianity. All Christian religions are affected by what transpires in Catholicism, even though many other Christian religions have denounced Catholicism, in some way or other. The roots of Catholicism are deep, and reach all the way back to Christ turning the keys of authority over to Peter. Therefore, what happens in Catholicism affects the entire Christian world, since all Christian religions are branches on the same tree.

There is a great awakening happening. If you are aware, and watch with your heart, you will be able to see the church of John, the Johannine stream, emerge, awaken, and come to life. It is possible that it may emerge out of any of the benevolent Christian religions, and will knit hearts together, unifying even across chasms of doctrinal differences. There must be unification in the Christian world. The church of John *is* love and unity.

This is the time for Catholics and Protestants to come together in true communion, each bringing their part of the body of Christ, and *together* they can become the body of Christ.

This is the work of Sophia, to gather all Her people—of all races, cultures, and religions in unification through compassion and tolerance for diversity. She does not ask for everyone to convert to one religion or one group. Every person brings value to the greater whole. And Sophia holds the space for all to come, to love one another, to listen, and to accept every part. This is how the true body of Christ is resurrected—when all of His faces, all of His hearts, all of His hands, and all of His feet can come together!

When the face of Catholicism and the face of Protestantism can behold the face of the true Christ in each other, then Christ is truly in the midst.

Many wars have been fought and are still being fought over doctrine. This is not Christ. He would not fight against Himself. He does not fight against those who are against Him. He is not present in those battles. He is in the pastures with the lambs who have gone astray. He is with the people who are sincerely searching for Him.

You find yourselves, because of your long histories in this world, having certain antipathies toward some religions, and sympathies with others. You have spent lifetimes experiencing different religions, philosophies, and doctrines. All the dogma, all the words, have amassed within your memory—until in this life, it becomes necessary to rise above, to free oneself from heavy dogma. Let Love be the religion. True religion is Love.

The Temple of Sophia is not the sanctuary of just one religion— one religion that has risen above the others, having achieved some higher status in the world's eyes, or is more perfect. The Temple of Sophia embraces all benevolent spiritual traditions. Sophia does not pick, and choose, and weigh one tradition against the others. She embraces all, and will hold all in the circle of Her Love until all is One.

Because of past experiences, some go running after this or that doctrine in order to pacify fears—fears of God, fears of judgment, fears of the afterlife. The thought is: *if I align with the right group who has the most truth, and the strongest leader, then I can find my way to the kingdom of God.* We feel the fragmentation that has happened in Christianity. Some are incessantly turning over every stone, looking for the pieces that can make a religion true and whole again.

See the *jewels* that are present in every religion. Those jewels are like holograms, pictures of the greater whole. They are Sophia's diamonds of Love. If one holds those jewels to the light, all colors ray out.

Sophia is not a divider, or a fragmenter. She is the Holy Begetress of the Good. All that is begotten by Her is of the original Good. Throughout time, all that She begot fell into division and fragmentation. Yet what originally existed, Her original creation, is not simply a memory, but continues to live in each and every heart.

Each heart is a part of the whole—the whole of Sophia's creation. To live in the embrace of Sophia is to feel one's self as part of the whole. It is to know one's self as Her beloved creation, and to see all people as Her begotten. She is the great unifier.

She will bring together and unify hearts. She will reveal the jewels of truth, beauty, and goodness that are present in every person, culture, and religion. When one is united with all, one dwells in paradise. Paradise is not just a future dream. It can manifest here and now.

Unification is the recollection of Sophia's original creation.

It is the remembering of what She begot in Love and Wisdom.

The holy women, who served Christ at the Turning Point in Time, are Sophia's priestesses. They guide us in this work of weaving back together the loosened, frayed, unraveled threads of the tapestry of creation.

All are blessed and have gifts. Claim these blessings, and She will give you the threads so that hearts may be restored and knit together in unity.

These words are given by the priestesses of Christ and Sophia, even those who walked as the holy women of Judea.

Amen.

How is Sophia working in our world situation—in every situation—today? Sophia is the ever-renewing Isis who calls us to live in a continual process of unveiling Her creation. Isis unveiled! To experience the unveiling of Isis is to come to know that She is a fecund goddess and to always remember Her fecundity. Life is a fertile field—upon which we are to learn to plant seeds and to work with Her fertility.

If Christ is the One whose seed She bears—"Not I, but Christ in me"—planting seeds would be to do deeds that are Christ-inspired. We live in Her body and She is fertile. We need to be careful what we plant. We need to take care daily to "weed the garden" and tend it. We are "swimming" in Her ocean of fertility.

—LACQUANNA PAUL
Journal for Star Wisdom, 2013

7

JOURNEY THROUGH THE ARCHANGEL

As the vision opened,[1] I saw an enormous angelic being that was so vast I knew it was an archangel. Within the core of this being was a brilliant white star; I felt the power of the archangel as its light penetrated my entire soul. Rays of effulgent colors and the tones of cosmic records suffused my soul. I saw Michael keeping the dragon at bay.

As I then passed through veils of light into the center of the archangel's being, a resonance I had never heard before emanated powerfully. Each wave of vibration caused an uplifting to occur throughout my being—a rising up of energy as if all of my cells were being turned upward to behold the Above. My soul was held aloft by divine breath.

I was then in a space of brilliant white light veils—and was still seeing the dragon subjugated by the sword of Michael. Michael held the dragon back, allowing me to pass through. Then an astonishing, surging force propelled me on, my very cells being drawn as if magnetically through a strong ray of white light. The resonance then changed, but this is difficult to describe. As I traveled on, eventually it was as if I were trying to fly into a headwind—I could feel how dense were the "cells of my soul," and this density caused resistance as I traveled. I could feel my cells cleansing and releasing so that the resonance would be able to merge with me, noticing the places where my soul had less light (due to

---

1   April 29, 2011.

unredeemed events of the past)—this is where the resistance was. The resonance seemed to be seeking out these places, to illuminate and purify them. During this time, I felt pinpoints of pain in my physical body. The cells in pain were "looking back" into the past from whence the darkness and density had originated.

Up ahead was cosmic space; and, far off in the distance, there was a rosy light. My heart yearned to go toward the rosy sphere. All the resistance that I was experiencing was then swept away— swept clean by the curious vibrations.

Continuing onward, I kept my focus upon the rosy light, which was astoundingly beautiful. Upon gaining closer proximity to it, I could hear the most soothing and melodious whispering tones. It was similar in vibration to the unconditional love of a mother who holds her infant, lovingly gazing into his eyes and whispering over and over, *I love you! Oh, I love you!* All around the rosy sphere were white wings moving gently, closing and opening in a rhythm like a heartbeat; it was from these wings of light that the whispering tones emanated. The whole of this ineffable sphere, with its wings and rosy light, resembled a cosmic rose. As I prepared to enter the sphere, I was cloaked in white light.

THE SPHERE OF THE COSMIC UNION
OF CHRIST AND SOPHIA

I then passed into the sphere of the union of Christ and Sophia—a place of *perfect love*. I beheld them sitting upon great thrones, crowned with radiant light. Their heart was One, and from this one heart radiated golden streams of light, the harmonies of which were the tones of their love. The seeds of their love, the seeds of creation, emanated forth in the golden rays of light. I was completely surrounded by the seeds of light—they hovered around me in space. I was able to gaze upon them, to see them up-close. They had a certain kind of consciousness, one that goes beyond any consciousness that can be found on the Earth at this time; and it was a consciousness that was different from other beings I have encountered as well. I was informed that they were the seeds of higher human consciousness, the *consciousness of future humanity*. The seeds of light were indescribably beautiful! It was like being surrounded by infant stars. Literally being birthed from the love of Christ and Sophia, they hovered all around. They were attracted to me, and interacted with me, very interested and curious about my form of being. I was in love and in a state of ineffable bliss, being in the presence of these cosmic "newborns!"

What happened next, I can hardly fathom!

Sophia, clothed in radiant rose-hued light, arose from Her throne. Her beauty was ineffable! Never could I do Her justice with mere words! Rosy light and harmonies and fragrances emanated from Her Being. Astonished and humbled by Her infinite love for humanity, I yearned to feel this same love. She removed her rosy light-mantle and placed it around my shoulders so that I could feel Her love for humanity. I was humbled to be able to feel, just for a moment, Her own motherly love for all creation: She sows the seeds of pure love; She weaves the consciousness of love. The consciousness of love is wisdom born of Her, for She is wisdom. To be given this gift was ever humbling—She is so good to us! How wonderful it is just to see and know and feel where humanity is headed in its evolution, being spiritually created and watched over by Christ and Sophia! If only we could all see humanity in this way and know that the seeds of this divine love reside within us! There would be only love, there would be no hate. Let us strive to see the seed of perfect union and harmony that is within each person we meet. We all have the power of love within us.

I received the love of Christ and Sophia. It was a holy parental love. There was no judgment for all the times I have gone astray. They love each of us unconditionally, mercifully. I was given time to simply be in silence with them, to receive their Love.

I wanted nothing more than to be the kind of mother that Sophia is. I do not know how I could ever be sufficient in my own self, able to radiate that kind of love to everyone, but this is my desire: to be on Earth and be a conduit for Christ's and Sophia's Love—to reflect the pure Love of Divine Union! To bring forth creation of higher consciousness, the consciousness of Love!

Sophia gave to me some of the rosy light from Her heart; it can grow within. *Our souls are lenses through which Her light can shine—we need only to keep the lens of our souls clean.* How wonderful it would be if everyone could know that they belong to Sophia, that She loves us so unconditionally!

The *harmonies* of the seeds of light are the codes for humanity's future state of consciousness, which is a consciousness of love. Having this light in one's aura can help to draw others toward a state of love. The light may illuminate what is *not* love in them, which could be painful as they come to know their own darkness and feel the need to release it, to cleanse and to purify. Although this is challenging and difficult, we all want to live in love. And so the darkness will be illuminated; then healing can be effectuated, and love will fill the spaces left by the fleeing darkness. The harmonies of the light contain the way. The way is Christ.

Lift up your hearts and be glad, for you are on your way to greater love. Live in love now. Be Love to all you meet. In everything that happens to you, ask yourself: how would Love act in this situation? What would Love do? Your efforts and desires to give and receive love, even the tiniest efforts, are enough for Christ and Sophia to work through, to touch human beings. Continually offer up your hate, your resistance, your bitterness. Free yourself. Go to the thrones of Christ and Sophia to offer up your darkness and ask them to return to you love, and joy, and compassion—and they will. They can perform a miracle in your heart. Instead of being angry at all the human beings around you who seem to be inept in loving others, lift all of it up to

Christ and Sophia and let go of it and allow Christ and Sophia to give you their love, that you may give it to others. Christ and Sophia love All. They love the ones who are hateful and angry and bitter just as much as they love those who are peaceful and kind and lighthearted.

Let go of trying to force love. The seeds of love are already within everyone. We cannot force love out of others. We cannot demand it. It would be like uprooting a fragile sprout out of the ground, to try to force it to be something bigger when it is not ready and not yet capable, when it has not even received the nourishment in order to grow. Allow the seeds of love to simply be in others. Nurture and cultivate those seeds. This means giving unconditional love, just as the Sun warms the Earth without choosing whether to warm this or that. Its rays of light are for all the Earth. The Sun is constant and loyal and ever present in predictable ways. There are times and seasons for the Sun. Trust in love. Love is ever present, like the rays of the sunlight. When you love those who seem so unlovable, you are nurturing the seed of love in them. As you go about doing your loving work, remember to always release the darkness you encounter to Christ and Sophia, who can transmute those vibrations for you.

I felt a tremendous strength, the strength of peace, the strength of love. I wanted to remain always in the presence of Christ and Sophia! I pray to always remember this love. I asked Christ and Sophia to protect it from whatever may try to take it away. In answer to this, they set the Archangel Michael over me as protection. As I asked for their love within me to be guarded by Michael, so it shall be. I must not forget to nurture their love within me. I must remember to ask for the protection of Michael.

I returned to Earth, passing again through the light of the archangel. I saw a radiant cross of light in the Earth, the reminder of Christ's love. It was so beautiful! Christ bled His love into the Earth. Christ's love is in the Earth—His love is here! This brought me such profound joy as I descended to the Earth, for I knew that none are separate from Him or His love.

He is here! I could feel Him and hear Him and see Him in all of nature throughout the whole Earth. I could hear the tones— the harmonies of His Presence emanating from the cosmos. They resound differently in the Earth than they do in the cosmos because the vessel holding the harmonies is different; and yet my soul recognized them. The harmonies of Christ resounded through me, the cosmic harmonies meeting the earthly harmonies. I passed through the cross of light as I returned to the Earth. I was so happy to be on the Earth! I love the Earth!

St. Christopher came to greet me. On this side of the River, I saw the Tree of Life with little buds of light on every branch. It reminded me of the seeds of light that I had seen when at the thrones of Christ and Sophia. We are all part of the Tree of Life; it is growing in us, and we are growing in it!

I am the first and the last
I am the honored one and the scorned one...
I am the wife and the virgin
I am the mother and the daughter
I am the members of my mother
I am the barren one, and many are her sons....
I am the silence that is incomprehensible
And the idea whose remembrance is frequent
And the word whose appearance is multiple
I am the utterance of my name.

—*The Thunder, Perfect Mind*
The Nag Hammadi Library

8

THE STARS OF HUMANITY

While in vision,[1] I saw a star radiating pure white light from within Christ's heart. I focused upon the star and realized that He was revealing my own star to me, being held within His expansive being! Drawn into the star of myself within His heart, I was then looking out from His heart, gazing upon the world. I gazed out from the "star that I am" upon the stars of all of humanity! The Earth was covered in beautiful stars. I felt Christ's immeasurable, never-ending love for all.

I saw a chasm between the stars of Heaven and the stars of humanity. The chasm was like a dark void around the Earth.

I descended through the chasm and witnessed the descent of the stars of humanity as they left Heaven to dwell on Earth. I felt the immense pain of having to separate one's star from the stars of Heaven. Each star, at one point, had passed through the Void, through the ostensible absence of the Divine.

Between Earth and the chasm, occluding the realm of Heaven, was the light of Lucifer surrounding the Earth. Its glow was a sickly light; it gave no life. I did not want to gaze upon it. The light of Lucifer causes us to lose sight of the stars that others *are*, fabricating illusions of temporal identities. Throughout our incarnations we become so full of pain and all the wrongdoings of our fellow humans against us that we then forget the star in the other.

---

1   June 18, 2009.

The pain causes us to go into an even deeper sleep, and our stars become *eclipsed* to one another.

I experienced great sadness as I saw how human beings have eclipsed the stars of others. It is my prayer that with this knowledge we may all do our best to serve the light of the other and work to bring the other's light to consciousness—to see the true light within and reflect it to all.

I knew that I had experienced the descent through that chasm several times.

I felt immense gratitude for Christ—that we are able to make amends for our misdeeds and be washed clean through His atoning sacrifice. Those whom we have harmed may return to us so that we may assist them, and we can recompense for our trespasses against them. We *want* them to return to us so that we can see the light in them be strengthened and renewed. As we help to magnify the light in others, we may present them to Christ as a gift for Him—a gift for His sacrifice.

In gratitude I spoke:

Oh Lord, I would bring every soul who has lost its way in the Earthly realm back to you, if I could! I want to show you my gratitude for Your sacrifice! This is the work that I want to do!

I looked into Christ's eyes; they were emanating the light of His Love. I put my hands up around His face and held His gaze. His face was majestically, inexpressibly beautiful. *You have known me, Lord, from whence I have come. You have known me since the beginning of my creation. And you know me in the future!* I felt the deep, reverential awe of being *known*.

THE TRANSFORMED EARTH

The transformed Earth of the future rose up before my vision; it was as if my face became the crystalline landscape of the glorified Earth. From the Earth, I was gazing up at the Cosmic Christ, who was beholding His fulfilled creation. My soul was in rapture, crying, *O My Holy, Holy, Holy Lord! It is finished! It is finished! It is fulfilled!*

And then I basked in the Silence of the transformed Earth. In the Silence dwelt the Eternal Word, who was from the Beginning and ever shall be. The Earth was held in the Silence; and the Silence is for all eternity. Sophia, who is Silence, was broken so that the Word could be born. When the Earth has reached its glorified state, then the Silence shall never again be broken. While being held in the Silence of the redeemed Earth, I experienced the past, present, and future Being of Sophia abiding in the glorified kingdom of Earth.

I then began to descend, enveloped in the divine love and mercy of the Sacred Heart of Christ.

Traveling through the stars, I saw the star of who I am, and it was through this that I reentered present time.

Saint Christopher assisted my return as usual.

What grief is borne by the Mother of Creation!
Silently and alone she hears her children crying out from the
Earth.
She bears the ancient grief of unshed tears,
Of the terrors of waters that sweep over whole peoples
driven into exile,
Hunted, humiliated, tortured, destroyed by other human
beings
Forgetful of their own dignity and responsibilities to others.
She stands on all this world's hills of sorrow.
As we continue to inflict the pain of hatred and vengeance,
greed and power on one another,
She bears her children's pain,
The rejection and fear of all Earth's exile.
Silently it screams with all those torn by hate's clawed hands.
She carries the sorrow of our inequity.

—KAREN RIVERS

9

THE ANGEL OF THE LAMB OF GOD SPEAKS

The voice of the Angel, who serves the Lamb of God, addressed me:[1]

You have created a sacred space in the Earthly plane to receive a special message—to bring word from the higher spiritual realm, which will go forth from this place now, to bless humanity, reaching the ears of those who are ready to receive.

The Lamb of God is in your midst, He who was slain for the sins of the World. Lay hold upon His sacrifice, which He fulfilled on your behalf and on behalf of humanity, and feel the great peace that knows no bounds.

O little flock, you are safely enfolded in Him! You hear His call and you come. You have proven yourselves worthy in times past and the Great Comforter is sent unto you. Indeed you have a very important mission to fulfill for the times that are coming.

All things are being prepared. A great vial shall be broken over the Earth and all who stand in the way of its vapors will be affected. Because of the fear generated by the Antichrist in the hearts of so many human beings, the angels will be held back for a moment, unable to impede the opening of this wrathful vial; darkness shall issue forth upon its breaking.

You find yourselves in the peace and calm before the storm. As darkness rolls forth upon the face of the land, there will be destruction and you shall see falling what used to be considered

---

1   I understood that the words of the Angel apply to any who receive this message. This communication was given on March 11, 2009.

57

great; and great shall be the fall of what was once mighty, and the reverberations of this fall shall reach your eyes and ears. You may experience the repercussion of this, but may not find yourselves under the direct impact of the fall.

Massive up-roaring waves shall abound; a great storm will ensue. And during this time, remember when Christ Jesus was asleep on the ship in the turbulent storm, and His disciples in great fear cried *Master, awaken!* They were terrified at the prospect of being tossed overboard by the waves, and they did the right thing and awakened the Master; He stretched forth his hand to the turbulence and said, *Peace, be still*. And the water became still.

During this tumultuous time you shall awaken the Master within yourself and shall perform the miracle of "calming the tempestuous seas."

Before this happens, there will be temptations to turn to other voices, whether they are within or without. Many voices shall say, "Lo here and lo there," offering some temporary gratification, but all they can offer are illusions, which can hold for only a moment if they have any power at all.

The Lord Himself can work through you. Trust and believe.

Just before He left his physical life on Earth, He gave a part of Himself, a seed of His Light—to each of the twelve disciples, that they might perform miracles. This did not come as an instant gift. They had to work with it and grow to understand it. They had to purify their need for power of any kind; but once they connected appropriately, they were able to call upon the gift in times of need, when it was an act of wisdom to manifest a work of God—and so their strength was then multiplied by Christ. Their gifts were multiplied so they could share the Christ with more people; and all who were touched and healed by them contain the seed of this power, which may be brought forth and illuminated—when the time is right. Each of you contains this seed within you to use for the healing and benefit of humanity. You will know when this seed of light has developed, and when it is time to use these gifts; and you will be shown how. You will be rays of light in the darkness and shall still the storm as you cleave to the Master.

Envision Him walking by your side, but also think of Him walking *within* you. His eyes become your eyes, His hands your hands, His feet your feet. This is the yoke of light wherein He is able to make burdens lighter. You will be astounded by how light you can feel while standing in the midst of turmoil.

You can become a Heaven and Earth; you can bear both within you. This may come about by passing through the turbulence and tribulation. This will not likely happen while you are engaged in discussing deep doctrine or doing mundane activities. The power manifests when it is needed; and you will fall to the Earth in gratitude when mighty works have been wrought through you.

These words are being given so you know that it is not always necessary to run into the wilderness and hide out of fear. Many shall do this and may be protected, but many who do this may not receive what can be received by willingly descending into the depths. And what shall be received by you will be carried forth and never forgotten, but will live on into your future incarnations.

So it is important that you receive this great gift and do not miss the opportunity. No matter what happens, you are enfolded in His flock, yoked to Him in the safe circle of His arms. It matters not that you do not fully know yourself or your gifts, for He sees through and He shall look upon you, and you will then see yourselves through His wondrous gaze.

The spiritual world stands in awe of you—that you would sacrifice your divine station and take up heavy crosses to serve humanity. This incarnation is a different one for each of you. It is one of a great work in times of world conflict; whereas previously you were gathering wisdom, knowledge, and light, you are now entering a field of *work*—and much of this work shall be wrestling with the darkness that comes.

The other miracle of Christ that can be brought forward now is the miracle of walking on the water. Not only did He calm the sea, but He also walked on the water. You must be willing to test the water of your faith by *walking out into what you have stilled*. This seems like an abstract idea but remember this image. You will not just calm the water but will need to *walk* on these waters. Meditate and work with this image.

Another aspect of this image is that you can rely on the beings of nature and the elements to support you. Have childlike faith, and even the weather shall respond to you. Children believe all things are possible, and indeed all things *are* possible. Even in the material world you can ask a mountain to be removed and it shall. You shall not need to remove actual mountains—but it is an enchanting idea for one whose faith is like that of a child!

Have faith in your ability to request and receive favors from the natural world. To the unawakened eye things can appear. In other words, if the adversary comes against you, you may have the ability to create something for the adversary, which causes the adversary to forget you. Be creative. What would a child do in certain situations? Children have fun with imaginations, in games of hide and seek.

This message is not given to cause fear; for, in a state of fear you have power to create only what you fear and little power to create viable solutions. If you can come to terms with the fears of pain and death, you can face an adversary from a perspective of love.

Remember the love you have for your heavenly home and the beings that know you and love you there; and this will carry you through so that you do not fall into fear; then you have the power to create what you choose to create. You shall even have the power to *love* the adversary you face and to see its purpose, its hidden value; and some adversarial forces can actually be transformed through your love, while others shall simply go away.

Perfect love casts out fear.[2]

---

2   1 John 4:18.

If you cannot connect to the heavenly love, there is a meditation that you may do. Place your gently closed fist over your heart chakra and with the other hand cover the fist and go within. Imagine the greatest human love you have ever known—and even if it pales in comparison to divine love, it is enough. For the seeds of divine love are planted in human hearts; and you have all received love from another human being. As you make this gesture over your heart chakra, and rest in that love, you will connect to a power of immunity. This not only activates the physical immune system of the body, but also activates immunity toward spiritual viruses, so to speak. Do this at the first instant you are aware you are being attacked spiritually. It is easier when the attack is "at the door."

The thymus is located over the heart and under the sternum. This place is like a door to the soul. You may literally tap on this place and speak the truth—that the door to Christ and His Peace may be opened to you. But this must be done by approaching in faith. *Knock in faith, and love shall be opened unto you.* Christ stands ready to open the door. And then shall you receive from Him.

You may also do this, etherically, for others. You may "knock" upon their door, so to speak, in love, and assist the opening of Christ to them. And, again, this is done only through love. For what you truly want to see is the Christ in the other. Seek for Christ in the other and you shall find. Ask for the Christ in the other and you shall receive. Knock and He shall be opened unto you.

This can happen with the most awful human beings that may come to you. This may happen without their knowing. They may feel only a subtle change. Even though some light of Christ may touch them, when they leave your presence they may go back to dark actions. However, many of them may lay down their swords and "pick up the plowshare" and join you in planting seeds of love into the dark soil, the soil of chaos. All chaos is fertile soil for seeds to grow.

Ugliness is the chaos of beauty; deception is the chaos of truth; evil is the chaos of good.

The Holy Lamb of God sends you forth amongst the chaos, standing firmly with feet in the fertile soil, planting the seeds that will grow into beauty, truth, and goodness. You are gardeners, sowers, tillers, reapers, and harvesters. You are love. And the sun and the living water and the breath of God shall work through you to nurture the seeds. You are nurturers of the Word; and a greater portion of the Word shall be given to you. Your voice shall become an instrument of the Word, and even your flesh may become the Word, as Christ dwells in you; and light shall come through you and touch all whom you meet.

And Sophia, the beautiful Bride, shall marry Herself to the Word within you; and you shall be filled with Her Silence, that the Word may be born; and the Word can be born only from the silence that She is. Embrace the Silence that will birth the Word. You must spend time in the Silence, just as you do in the Word. She is the Silence that shall deliver the Word, and She shall lead you to a land of milk and honey; even in the midst of the turbulence, you will find the places of milk and honey, places of sweetness and rest. And She shall lead you there.

Sophia loves all her children, good or evil. All are within Her loving embrace. She does not cast judgment, but calls all to Her; and in the work of Sophia we call our brothers and sisters home to Her heart to be held within Her *Pietà*.[3]

All souls, when incarnating on this Earth, made a great sacrifice and laid down what they knew. The greatness of themselves they sacrificed; and many are coming here to play certain roles on the stage of humanity, roles that appear horrible and ugly. She is able to see beyond the costumes and love them still; and She can teach this to you. You will find in your arms (spiritually speaking)

---

3   The author has often experienced the Blessed Virgin holding souls in her arms in the gesture of the *Piéta*, as depicted in Michelangelo's great work, *The Piéta*.

some of these sacrificial humans who will lay down their lives so that the purposes of God can be accomplished on Earth. And some of these individuals may be the most vile and ugly apparitions of evil; and I use this word—apparitions—because that is what they will be. For, indeed, all that is Luciferic, all that is Satanic, is illusion. You will learn to hold them in your arms as if they are the Christ Child. Pray for Sophia to reside with you in those moments, to hold them in Her arms; for She would call them home like the prodigals. She rejoices in this great work.

I have given you many words to buoy you up through the times of trial. You are called to this work by the spiritual world. This is not, as you know, given to you to arrogate yourselves, but is given to you because it is a fulfillment of a promise promulgated before you came here. Destiny is being fulfilled as we speak, for Christ and Sophia are gathering their forces and preparing them. There are others like you. Some you shall meet, others you will not. What is being done now, here, is being done in other places in the world. You are part of a great whole.

Connect now with your spiritual community, which is spread throughout the world. Embrace your community. They are embracing you also. A great web of love is forming around Earth, and wherever you walk—that is holy ground. You take that connection wherever you go.

Maintain this connection with your community. Become aware of the beings that serve this spiritual community, who are gathered in the "atmosphere" of this community.

All is held within the loving and watchful embrace of Christ and Sophia; you are beheld by them—and this beholding is for all time and for all eternity.

Peace, be still.

Amen.

Our Earthly Mother,
She who sends forth her Angels
To guide the roots of man
And send them deep into the blessed soil.

We invoke the Earthly Mother!
The Holy Preserver!
The Maintainer!
It is She who will restore the world!

The Earth is hers,
And the fullness thereof the world,
And they that dwell therein.

—ESSENE GOSPEL OF PEACE, BOOK 2
(Translated by Edmond Bordeaux)

10

THE HOLY WOMEN SPEAK OF SOPHIA

After praying, and requesting to commune with the holy women who followed Christ Jesus when He lived on the Earth, I saw a sphere of radiant light in which all colors were present. Ethereal warmth radiated from the light and I saw a circle of spiritual sisters—twelve women encircling three in the center.

They conveyed the following message[1]:

We were drawn to the Son of God when we lived in Judea. Christ Jesus was the perfect Man. There was nothing in Him that would subordinate women. Never did He cause the women to feel less important than the men who followed Him. From time to time we struggled with this new paradigm, and also with jealousy that arose within us. We had never known a man who loved and honored women so perfectly. Some of us had little or no self-worth when we met Him—but through our association with Him we found our worth.

It was not just the way that He talked, or His mannerisms—we simply felt known and loved by Him. He could "see" us. The divine love between Him and His Blessed Mother was the same love we eventually knew with Him.

We were chosen before we incarnated as representatives for all women to bring the universal pain of women to Christ for healing. This was one aspect of our work. Each one of us carried an aspect of the universal suffering of the feminine gender, and each one of

---

1   This occurred on May 1, 2011.

us received healing. Together we were the template for the healing of universal feminine suffering. This suffering may be healed through Christ, who came to heal all things.

Our work and the stories of our healings have been veiled for almost two millennia. Even though we have revealed our stories to others in times past, our stories have not yet come to mainstream awareness; and yet the keys for the healing are there.

In the coming times our veils will be lifted and we shall tell our stories and reveal how the universal pain may be healed through Christ. For Christ is the Bridegroom who shall come again, and Sophia is His Bride; and Sophia calls to Her daughters: *Come and be healed, that you may go out and heal others!*

And Sophia's Daughters of Light are the ones who hear Her voice as She descends from the starry realms. There are those who hear Her voice and awaken to this universal pain, and strive for healing.

Sophia is coming!

Offer up your pain and heartache as a work of suffering that you do for the universal feminine. Your grief and unworthiness and despair are the pain of the universal—seek to heal your own life as a blessing for all. You are the microcosm of the macrocosm. Those who are in female incarnations at this time are playing an integral role, for it is a time of great awakening.

The Evil One, the dragon, is indeed agitated and roused. The dragon wants to stop humanity from awakening; for within every human heart that has awakened to the true light, the union of Christ and Sophia within the heart becomes possible. Those hearts shall then become the "womb" from which the male child shall be birthed[2]; but the dragon wants to stop *every* human heart from awakening to Sophia as She is descending, to thwart the union of Christ and Sophia in human hearts.

---

2   See also Rev. 12:5.

Be at peace. Once the heart awakens, it will never go back to sleep. Do not fear, for you have been given the power to crush the dragon's head. You must be alert and prayerful to maintain the spiritual protection, which is strengthened through purity and healing. Ask for protection from Archangel Michael, who is well acquainted with the dragon.

Some are forerunners in preparing for Sophia's coming. Indeed it is a difficult task to be a forerunner. You may want to cling to the past. You are not a creature of the past, but of the future. Do not *dwell* in the future but live in present time and be aware of the time that is just a step ahead. If you cling too much to the past, you are not able to do your work and receive what is coming.

You must be empty grail vessels so that the Grail King can call forth sustenance from you to nourish others. *If your cup is too full already, you are unable to receive. Spiritual sustenance can come through only you if you remain an open channel.*

Each soul is an individual with its own path. In times past there were individuals who had strong missions to set things in motion by assertively exerting their will forces—and likewise today some are called to use their voices to effectuate change. Quite often forerunners feel a strong need to help bring about the future they see coming.

If you know that you have a strong calling to use your voice for change, then this is your path. You must *know* your path.

Most forerunners are quite alone. They lead humanity by pure consciousness and vision—as well as through advancing on the path of individual inner purification and development.

Focusing on the good is absolutely essential. You must focus on the good to increase it. Focusing on what seems wrong or hateful causes divisiveness, contention, and drama. If you do not approve of something, then focus upon and strengthen the good—while reducing the focus on what is wrong.

Your work is with the good unless you have been called by a higher being to work in transforming evil, or in uplifting darkness. If you are not told in a *strong* way, it is not time for you. Those called in such a way have the requisite spiritual protection. Those not called are oftentimes doing this work to satisfy their own egos; and they may not have the protection they need, other than what they can give themselves.

The times in which you now live in are exciting for us to behold. For what we began as our work 2,000 years ago is now taking shape and blossoming at this Second Coming of Christ—and you are a part of this work. Seek to know Christ; seek for healing through Him. Such is the path we walked then. And for you to do your work now, you must walk that path of healing in Christ. Then shall the work of the holy women be multiplied in you and made manifest in profound ways.

We are working through you to prepare hearts to receive Sophia. We shall be guiding you.

One loses protection when one is led off the path. This happens in infinite and subtle ways. There must be mindfulness. Most often it is in relationships with others that you may be led away from your true path. The Evil One will try to pull down relationships that are Sophianic *first and foremost*. There is strength in numbers—wherever two or three are gathered together in Christ, there is protection. The Evil One engenders egocentricity—or unworthiness—so that people will want to isolate themselves away from spiritual community. He shall use very subtle tricks to divide spiritual friendships asunder.

We want to address another aspect of "forcing the future": Be on guard with your speaking, that you do not give precious gems of light to people who do not have the vessels to receive; for they will lose the light or fling these gems back at you, distorted, and may even try to persecute you. Because of the times you are in, you must be circumspect with the words you use. The word has the power for good and for evil. One must let go of the need for everyone else to jump on board with your plans, or to join you in conscious community. Those who are ready will come. Be glad for the ones who come. Do not be drawn away from your true path by a sense of sorrow for those who do not yet resonate with your community. Let go of the fear that would cause you to believe that if you are not proselytizing you are not saving souls—everything the world is going through is bringing the world closer to joy.

Human beings are going through what they need to in order to come to greater joy. See your words as precious gems of light. Use them with conscious intention. It is a challenge to watch one's words, but it is important to know that the power to create is becoming more and more potent through words.

It is also a challenge to see and know truth and not exert change. With the increase of gifts, comes greater suffering. With greater consciousness, comes greater sorrow.

Forerunners must allow others to be where they are and not judge them, but accept and love all.

The spirit world appreciates human work. Even the most mundane tasks, when done with singleness of heart, serve the spiritual world. For when you perform mundane tasks, you can bring a resonance to future humanity. By means of those tasks you then leave an imprint of consciousness upon the work you do—which imprint will change things and inform the future. Harm can be done if you enter into such things and see them as beneath you, as wrong—if you go into resentment and judgment. You imprint that into the situation—you really do leave your mark on the world. It is a true ideal to "receive enlightenment and then chop wood." Bring your love into whatever task you do and you shall make your mark with higher consciousness, blessing the generations who come after you.

Again, there are some who are called to use their voices; and they must know that they are called to use their voices to effect outer change. We as holy women could not use our voices much at all. You each are now able to use your voice more than we ever could, but the question is how to use your voice. We would have wanted to run and shout *He is Risen!* And we tried, but were silenced. Instead, we had to take that proclamation and bury it and carry it in our hearts. But our testimonies live in the etheric atmosphere of the world and shine as a brilliant light for all to see who have the eyes to see!

We left an indelible imprint upon the world: *that we knew and saw the dead arise from the grave!* And though our voices went veritably unheard (except for Martha, who became a great teacher, the rest of us did not have great audience); our voices are now arising from the dust—there are some who speak for us now.

Be at peace, for truth lives forever. Truth carried in the heart is indeed serving the world. Speak when you are given to speak and be silent when you are given to be silent. Through Silence, the Word is born.

All is well. We are yet working through you and are grateful to leave this message with you.

This is a most beautiful work; Sophia is at the head of this work!

✿

In light of the fact that Mary Magdalene was one of the holy women, it seems appropriate at the end of this chapter to include the following excerpt from the trilogy Through the Eyes of Mary Magdalene. *This passage is from chapter 33 of volume 3.*

[The individuality of Mary Magdalene is] a bridge between the first coming of Christ and the second coming. Her work as Mary Magdalene also laid the foundation for humanity to receive Holy Sophia in a far distant, future time, when She will make Her glorious descent toward the Earth. Magdalene has been weaving between these most important events, preparing the Earth and its inhabitants to receive Christ in His second coming—and to then receive Sophia, the consort of Christ. *We can say that Magdalene is one who works to unite Christ and Sophia in the hearts of humanity.*

The marriage of the Lamb and His Bride can take place in the human heart! Magdalene is the priestess of this holy sacrament, but she does not bring it in the way that some people in certain movements would claim that she does. Much mystery has surrounded the concept of the union of the divine masculine and feminine. It will remain a mystery until hearts are prepared to enter into this divine sacrament in the way it was truly intended. And although not many are ready to receive it at this time, the world is being prepared for a time when this will be possible for ever more people.

One can have Christ and Sophia wedded within oneself only if one is truly pure in heart. The true union of divine masculine and feminine can never come about in an impure heart. There exists a counterfeit experience that is not so difficult to come by. The road to counterfeit union, so to speak, is paved with many subtle temptations along the way.

Until one has undergone soul purification, one has not the power of divine union. This power is gained through *moral integrity*. Morality is power! Through contemplating the life of Magdalene, an understanding can arise that, only through moral uprightness, one may become a vessel for inflowing grace and spiritual power. Even those who have been the most pure are subject to temptations. Even while they strive to understand the divine within them, to experience union with the divine—they can fall. There are those who hardly succumbed in the past, but who can now be led astray; for the wiles of Lucifer and Satan are so clever and so subtle that one can indeed be deceived in ever more ways. One can think that there has been an illumination—and yes, Lucifer's light indeed illuminates the soul—but it is a flash that cannot endure, and the soul is then left hungry for more. Thus the soul is led away into paths that are morally catastrophic.

The only sure way to know that the path is true is to strive with all one's might to keep one's self in that straight and narrow way—that tiny thread that leads to eternal life—and to protect one's integrity and virtue as if one's very life depends upon one's virtue remaining whole!

Much has been twisted and distorted in Magdalene's name. She saw that this would indeed come to pass.

She will come especially to guide those who realize that they bear darkness within, and who awaken to the consequences of their choices and cry out for deliverance. She will not come to those who say in her name: "All is well. Let us eat, drink, and be merry!" She comes to those who admit they have fallen. She is their loving companion who leads them to Christ, and prepares them to attend the marriage of the Lamb and His Bride.

In Eastern Christian thought there lives a remarkable figure.
This figure is Mary, the Mother of God,
who is at the same time Sophia, the Holy Wisdom.
She is also the "Church,"
the principle of the community of all humanity,
And is therewith of the same essence with Christ.
The principle is therefore the principle of community (ecclesia);
That is, what unifies all Beings.

—VALENTIN TOMBERG

II

THE POWER OF SOPHIANIC COMMUNITY

In April 2007, while working in a healing capacity with a dear friend, a being appeared to me and answered questions that had been coming up during the course of our session. We were working together in a meditative way, looking into the energy of pain that was in my friend's body, and with the goal to discover the cause (which was emotional in nature) and then work with the energy to bring about resolution. The being was definitely feminine in nature, and showed herself in the image of a beautiful, delicate red flower with many layers of petals of light. We immediately felt great love emanating from her, and found that she was very interested in our healing work. We were led into deeper ways of healing the soul through her guidance. She eventually revealed more about herself to us, and told us that we could refer to her as "Etherium." In December of that same year, almost exactly three months before I had a profound and enduring experience of Christ's stigmata, Etherium spoke of the need to cleanse the blood, and to prepare for great changes to happen in the blood, giving me much guidance in that regard. She also further introduced herself with these words:

I am she who arose from the dust of Gethsemane and counted every drop, and I called every drop by its own name, and every drop is known by me. Every drop is restored to that Mighty Sufferer, and Holy is His Name. Oh, Precious Drops of Sacrificial Love—this is the name of my spirit! Like the condensation that occurs, bringing every drop back to the great ocean, I am that condensation of every drop. Oh, precious, precious Blood!

Etherium has visited me and others many times over the course of the past few years, bringing her gentle guidance and solace in times of great suffering—revealing ever more about herself, little by little. On July 27, 2010, Etherium gave a wonderful description of herself, which I include here:

It is I, Etherium. I come to you through the light of the Christ that is present in the etheric sphere around the Earth. I want to say something by way of introduction, of the being that I am, for those who do not yet know me. I came into being on a certain level when Christ's blood spilled into the Earth, beginning during the night of Gethsemane and culminating with the last drop that fell from the Cross. As the Being of Christ merged more and more into the body of Jesus of Nazareth, the more His blood became etherized thereby—it became spiritualized. The drops of blood that fell into the Earth contained the lifeblood of the Christ. This etheric blood, embodied by the physical blood of Jesus, was carried into the Earth, and the merging of this blood with the Earth—the Earth's physical and etheric bodies—gave birth to the being that I am. I am the being of this merging. In a sense you could refer to me as a nature being, from the aspect of my origin in the Earth. There is also a cosmic aspect to my being, which hails from a much higher sphere. I give voice to the Christ Being, who has merged with the Earth. Essentially, what I speak to you comes from the body of Christ, which is the Earth. I am deeply connected to all forms of blood: that of the human, animal, and plant kingdoms—the fluids that give life.

With this introduction, I now bring to you Etherium's message on Spiritual Community, which was given on September 28, 2010:

I shall speak once again regarding the state of the World Soul as it stands. I am pleased that you have gathered together to bring forth this message and am pleased that you are reaching out to bring others into your circle of work, to create a community of spiritual people who will be able to strengthen and edify each other; and not only this, but also to become a living vessel wherein the Holy Soul may do its work—not only within your *individual* souls, but also within the souls of the community you are forming, which shall then ray out into the World Soul.

Those of you who are coming together in spiritual community are being called to do so, and each of you brings to community strengths and weaknesses, dispositions and personalities, ideas and philosophies, as well as your experiences and talents; and not one of you is strong enough on your own, and not one of you is intelligent enough on your own, and not one of you is powerful enough on your own. It takes a community to bring out the *highest* in each of its members. Without community there is little growth or progression.

Now, as there are evil "communities" on the Earth—evil communities that were formed long ago, and those being newly formed even now—they are not to be feared, for the axiom *"where two or three are gathered together in my name, there am I in your midst"* does not pertain to communities formed with evil purposes. A higher being does not overlight such groups. These communities are formed by egotistical individuals who maintain their separateness and their own position, even within the so-called community. Such individuals do not sacrifice themselves—their own desires or their identities—for the sake of the whole. Such groups do not need to be feared because they are not cohesive in the spiritual sense. These groups only appear to be communities, but in actuality they are mere collections of individuals who are separate from one another, essentially standing alone. Thus there is a great weakness.

The gift of a righteous community is that individuals may actually increase in truth, beauty, and goodness as they sacrifice for the whole. By *sacrifice* I mean to say that they become empty and transparent—in that they do not require other members of the community to adapt to their own ideas or their own ideals. They allow sharing. They allow differences, and diversity. They allow for all the various colors of the rainbow to be present. For only through acceptance can there be unity. This is the gift of the Holy Soul, at this point in history when there are "evil communities" on the Earth, communities that appear to be falling apart, and communities rising up against one another.

The Holy Soul is now working through twelve communities of Light. These are not communities bound by color, nationality, philosophy, or religion. These are etheric communities; as these communities come together, being called by the Holy Soul, the individuals who join them will be blessed through their associations within those communities with greater knowledge and wisdom and goodness and with truth and beauty—far beyond what they could receive on their own.

Each individual person in the community is a microcosm of the community itself, as well as of an even greater macrocosm— the Soul of the World, the Earth and its inhabitants.

We can say that the individual body is like a community in and of itself, where organs and glands and various systems need to be able to perform their own functions while working in community with the rest of the body. What is done outwardly in the greater community with which one is involved is mirrored in the individual's body and soul. Essentially, such individuals will enter into communion with their own self. This means that they eventually learn to love their self, to accept their self. This is a great gift and was the wish of Christ Jesus when He said, *"Love thy neighbor as thyself."* We must first love ourselves so that we may love one another. The Holy Soul works the miracle of love within community, and draws out from the individual his or her gifts and capabilities so that the entire community is blessed by the presence of each individual person.

Individuals who join in spiritual community may be empowered and inspired as to what they can do in answer to the issues currently affecting the World Soul. In true community each individual can be held in the right way, whereby no one person is above another, but all are able to bring their gift—and all are deemed worthy.

Remember that the power you have against the forces of evil is community. *Community is the power.* It is by belonging to a community that you truly become a disciple of Christ. There is a great strength that weaves between all members of the community, a strength that those evil groups do not have. As you enter into community, your hearts will be connected to one another. There will be a weaving that will happen between hearts, so that hearts are knit together into one great heart. And as Christ is the center of such communities, He enters into the heart of each one of them, so that it becomes *His* heart. These communities are thereby imbued with great light and peace and love and protection.

Eventually these communities may become physical places. The individuals may then be called to physically join themselves in community to a particular location, in order to fortify a physical place in the Earth. They become fortresses of spirit, fortresses of love. And the way will be provided as to how this can happen; and the power to this end comes through the strong heart of the community.

Presently, the great war of the Middle East has been spiritually created, as it were. The enmity is already there. The ideas have already been generated—the plans for destruction. If you could see into the spiritual realm, you would see that the war has already begun. It is already raging.

But you may also turn your inner gaze and look at what is being created in the spiritual realm through the power of the Holy Soul. This can bring hope—a great hope. The angels are already working, because of the prayers and desires of righteous humans to create spiritually the *antithesis of war*, which is community, blessed *Christed community*. For war is anti-community. And the evil being that brings about war is the evil *counterpart* of the Holy Soul, which will not be addressed at this time. Those who are working through the Holy Soul are countering the workings of that evil one. But realize that there is great spiritual creation happening that goes beyond what can be experienced through the physical senses.

Some of you may ask: "*What is the remedy for war?*"

And I say to you: "**You are the remedy—you who belong to a spiritual community are the remedy for war.**" In times past, throughout history, there have been spiritual communities who were protected from war, from the pillaging, from the evil; and it was not only because they prayed; protection occurred also through the *power* of community. The community itself becomes a protective field when its individuals are acknowledged, accepted, and loved. Of course there were spiritual communities that suffered greatly, were violently disbanded, and even killed—the Apostles, for instance. This was to serve a higher purpose; for there was a greater purpose in the physical community being taken into the spiritual realm. When it happened, it was necessary; and there is much more to this mystery that will not be focused upon at this time.

As hearts become attuned to one another, what is being created spiritually will begin to manifest more in the physical—and shall counter what is being created by the Evil One.

Trust that you are loved! You are being watched over. You are beheld by the loving eyes of the spiritual realm. You will be brought together and your prayers will create a new Earth. Take these words into prayer. The spiritual world is calling you to serve the greater community of humanity by entering into spiritual community.

Amen.

You have bid me build a temple on your holy mountain
and an altar in the city that is your dwelling place,
a copy of the holy tabernacle that you had
established from of old.
Now with you is Wisdom, who knows your works
and was present when you made the world;
Who understands what is pleasing in your eyes
and what is conformable with your commands.

Send her forth from your holy heavens
and from your glorious throne dispatch her
that she may be with me and work with me,
that I may know what is pleasing to you.

—WISDOM OF SOLOMON, 9:8–10

12

Sophia and the Rose of the World

The following vision[1] took place at a sacred Nature temple space, which I was visiting with some friends.

On the temple grounds, we began with a prayer eurythmy[2] sequence.[3] There is a portion to this practice wherein the words of Christ are spoken while performing certain gestures. I experienced Christ's Presence most profoundly during the part wherein the words of the Risen One, the Resurrected Christ, are invoked.

After this, we began a walking meditation, encircling the Temple grounds three and a half times while singing *Kyrie Eleison, Christe Eleison, Sophia Eleison* (3½ times to honor the years of Christ's ministry). I enjoyed the meditation very much. However, to my utter astonishment, when we turned to face the center of the grounds at the end of the meditation, I saw something I had never seen before: with my physical eyes, I could see into another dimension! This truly defies description; I had never experienced this before—in the *physical* realm. It was as if the temple grounds had transformed into a dome of very high-vibration frequencies,

---

1   February 12, 2012.

2   Eurythmy is a spiritual path based on movement, much in the way that yoga and qigong are movement-based spiritual paths. Eurythmy means "beautiful, harmonious movement"; see the foreword in Powell, *Cultivating Inner Radiance and the Body of Immortality*.

3   The sequence *Putting on the Resurrection Body* is described in Powell, *Cultivating Inner Radiance and the Body of Immortality*, which also describes the eurythmy gestures for Universal Love and for the sound "M," referred to later in this vision.

which appeared as a shimmering mirror-like edifice. This was similar to the way that a mirage appears, silvery and shimmery, but the energy was not moving in waves—it was stable.

Around this dome were twelve portals, one to each of the zodiacal constellations. I could see through the portals—some of them appeared to be "open" and others were "closed." There was one in particular that was wide open and beckoning: the portal to Cancer.

I turned around to look at my friends and they were now as if *one being*. They seemed, moreover, to be completely at one with the land, and the land was at one with them. One friend spoke to me, and it was as if the land itself was speaking through her. I was unsure of what to do next. Another friend offered that I could go ahead and experience whatever it was that was happening, and perhaps they each could experience it through me.

I took in a breath and turned back to the center of the circle. I then saw a portal open between the doors to Cancer and Leo. It looked like the entrance to a cathedral; but rather than of stone, it was fashioned out of the elements of Nature. In the center of the opening was a being that stood in the form of a cross. I then saw that the being itself *was* the portal. I knew I was looking into another dimension, and that this being was a guardian for Heavenly Sophia, guarding the womb of her heart. I remained at this threshold for quite some time.

Then I looked around and saw that there were twelve enormous golden beings standing in a circle. They were huge! They were like worlds in and of themselves and were facing the center of the circle in a strong "M" (eurythmy gesture) with their hands at the level of their chests, palms facing forwards, as if they were pushing against something. I understood that they protect and guard the space and time where Sophia dwells. As far as the human being is concerned, Sophia dwells outside of space and time—no human being can penetrate to "where" She is unless the guardians allow it.

While at the threshold, I wanted to be with Sophia. The guardians do not allow any to pass who try to approach from a state of fullness. I made my request to see Her from a state of emptiness. The guardians stepped back, making the gesture of Universal Love, with arms outstretched as if to embrace, and radiating warm golden light—it was the same quality of light I have seen in Shambhala.

The guardian beings were very different from the one being I saw as the portal to Sophia. The twelve beings were huge and warm, like suns. I understood that they were very powerful cosmic beings that had been called to serve Shambhala, and that since they had sacrificed themselves to serve in this capacity, they had changed and transformed.

Through Christ opening the way to Shambhala, these beings are able to evolve along with Earth's evolutionary process. These beings have been guarding the aspect of Sophia that descended, and have something to do with Will. Indeed, unless human souls undergo a purification of the will, these beings remain immovable for them. *When purified, the will forces are in complete service to the Divine, and they become thereby the forces of Love.* Purified Will is the power of Love, in the sense of Love as a *verb*. If one's will is simply to follow one's own agenda, these beings seem unapproachable, impenetrable. When in the "M" gesture, they appear like golden statues, guarding with the strength of a very protective mother who will do all that she can to protect her children. It is only through Love—when the will is transformed into Love—that they then appear in the Universal Love gesture, holding their arms open and radiating the golden light of Divine Love. As they open up in this way to allow a person to pass through, they look like angels and take on their more cosmic appearance.[4]

---

4   I cannot say that my will has reached a state of complete purification. Perhaps I have been allowed to see Heavenly Sophia in order to teach others about Her.

The other being, who appeared as the portal to Sophia, was a reflective being—like a mirror. If one is full of self, then one cannot know that the being is there—for it reflects one's self, and there is then a struggle with what is reflected. It shows itself as a portal only when one is empty, and then the being appears as a silvery, shimmery portal who grants access. Until one is empty, the reflection of the self will occlude the portal to Sophia, as this being is both a mirror and a portal—and if one gets caught in the mirror aspect, one does not know it *is* a portal. The being does not *call* to you. Your soul *yearns* for it. And yet you cannot at first find this being, precisely because it does mirror: the closer you draw to it, the more you see your own reflection and notice something about yourself. If you become stuck in what you see about yourself, you will see only your reflection and not notice the portal.

When you are full of self, this being is rather fiery; but when you are empty, it is cool and silvery, and brings clarity.

One must first go through the Cross in order to approach Sophia.

Returning to the twelve guardians: I saw them in cosmic space making the Universal Love gesture. Sophia then descended into the center of their circle, Her robes radiant with prisms of light and swirling around Her in space. She was clothed in a starry mantle. Her face was luminous white like a pearl.

I was in awe as I saw Her take up a strong stance of love and strength—the stars all around Her were mirroring Her might! I could feel Her strength and power in the twelve guardians. She held a sword in Her right hand and a chalice in Her left. She raised the sword to a horizontal position across Her shoulders, while She held the chalice at the level of Her womb, the bowl of the chalice positioned in front of Her heart.

She said, holding out the chalice: *I shall receive whom I shall receive. But those whom I cannot receive will not be allowed to approach!*

It then occurred to me that She was showing "the blade and the chalice"—an image of the union of the divine masculine and feminine energies. In the chalice was the offering of Herself. She held out the chalice and lowered the sword and said, *Come and partake of Me, that I may dwell in you and you in Me.*

As She extended the chalice, it multiplied to become many chalices—enough for all to partake of the milk and honey of Her Grace and Love. I tasted the milk and honey, and then She gazed lovingly into my eyes. Time passed, but I do not know how much time....

When I opened my eyes, I saw that the entire space of the temple grounds was filled with the Light of the milk of Her grace. I was again astounded by the light that I could see with my own eyes!

I heard Her speak: *My body is the Silence. I give to you my radiant garment of Light. You are the garment of My Being; you are all the body of My Being!*

Beckoned, I went toward Her to receive Her and entered into Her Silence. Her robes opened: within Her Being were the starry heavens in Holy Silence. I felt the stars imprint themselves on the garment of my being so that I was *clothed* in Silence; I became the Silence.

After this, I saw Sophia again, standing upon a luminous rose. The petals started to fall away from the rose and fly through space. With the petals of Her rose, I traveled through time and space, seeing the annals of time pass by me on either side. I understood that the "Rose of the World" was once held in oneness, but separation occurred and eventually manifested as various and sundry religions and philosophies divided against each other.

I again saw Her standing upon this Rose and watched the petals tear from the Rose, as if tearing out from Her own heart. I saw the petals fall into our own hearts! We—the lovers of Sophia— carry the petals of her Rose in our hearts! We carry the petals of past, present, and future. We had been an important part of the process by which the separation occurred, having incarnated at various times while bearing her petals in our hearts. We had tasks that we accomplished within the different religions and philosophies of the world, and thus have carried the petals of the Rose of the World in our hearts for a long time.

Sophia suffered a tearing away; as human beings defined and limited God in their finite minds, these petals were torn from Her heart and scattered by the "winds of doctrine."

But She has watched over each and every petal that has fallen from the Rose of Divine Wisdom.

And we each have a divine mission to care for the petals within our own hearts until it is time for the Rose of the World to manifest in its wholeness.

The Rose of the World, once restored, shall become the chalice where all may partake of Sophia's Wisdom; all shall receive of Her and be nourished.

She wants us to become aware of the precious petals that we each bear within us. We are a part of Her great hope, Her plan for the New Earth. Each one of us is the Rose of the World, for we bear the Rose within us! We are the microcosm of the Rose—the Rose that will become the Rose of the World!

She told me that we are a *Star*. Together, we are the being of a Star.

When I opened my eyes again, I beheld Her radiant garment of light touching everything around us! Every tree, every flower, the birds, and each one of us—were clothed in Her radiant garment! We were in Her and She in us!

Remembering the awe-inspiring image of Sophia with the sword and chalice, I searched to find a depiction of any goddess who might appear this way. I was excited to find the photo (next page) of a monument that has graced the capital of the nation-state of Georgia since 1958, the 1,500th anniversary of Tbilisi.

Tbilisi Mother Georgia

Standing on the top of Solokai Hill overlooking Tbilisi, *Kartlis Deda* (the Mother of Kartli) wears traditional Georgian dress and is 20 meters tall. In her right hand is a sword, to defend against enemies, and in her left is a bowl of wine to greet all friends of Georgia. Kartlis Deda's pose is slightly different from the one I saw Sophia hold, but the message is so very similar!

Divine mother, Divine Son,
wellsprings of unending love, unending acceptance,
unending spiritual renewal, together placing
the archetype of resurrection in the light
into the physical world so that there might be the possibility
for the Birth of Light in the souls of all human beings
throughout the world, 2,000 years later.

—Nancy Jewel Poer

13

THE SEED OF THE RESURRECTION BODY

I saw Christ coming toward me, surrounded by all the stars of the heavens.[1] He was glowing with such a brilliant white light that I could see just His eyes, His smile, and His hands and feet.

He came toward me and opened His robes to show me the wound in His side. Then He showed me each of His other wounds. Lastly He showed me His Sacred Heart.

He said, *This is the Holy Grail.*

I beheld the starry script of the Grail flowing out from His Heart. It completely enveloped the space around me. I saw that the starry script is inscribed in every heart! It is in each one of us! I was in a state of profound awe because *every single person was a star in the starry script,* and the starry script is not complete without all of us—every person.

Then Christ descended toward me, and stood on the Earth, directly in front of me. His priestly robes were blue-violet, and His hair was like gold. His eyes were blue rays of light.

He opened His robes and I beheld all the stars of the heavens— all the stars were gazing upon the peoples of the Earth.

Then I saw Him approach various people, walking right up to them, beholding them, revealing the stars to them. He beheld the star of each person.

He showed me a special place that was completely surrounded by shining white veils. He led certain souls to this place, and laid them down.

---

1   This vision occurred on May 20, 2013.

Then He called upon Sophia. She appeared in white priestess robes, shimmering in silvery rays. She was like a priestess bride.

Christ directed Her to take each soul, and She held the soul in Her arms in the *Pietà* gesture. Together they beheld the dying of each soul—each dying to its own self. Christ anointed each while She held the soul in Her arms.

I experienced this in my own soul—with them gazing into my eyes. It was the most precious thing that I ever saw—their eyes gazing into mine! Then I saw them beholding everyone in that way. I saw certain people who were either going through a death or were on the verge of it.

Christ and Sophia want everyone to know: *We are holding you; We are beholding you while you are suffering and dying.*

At one point, while Sophia was holding a soul in its dying state, Christ stood up and moved toward me. In His hands was the *seed of life*. He opened his hands, and I saw the resurrection body of each soul unfold from His hands like a dove with brilliant wings. I saw the resurrection body being held and prepared for each person. Christ and Sophia are standing right next to us! They are holding our resurrection body for us!

I saw each soul rise up, emanating pure love. Then I saw each of these countless souls receive their garment of light, and become clothed in that light.

THE EARTH IN ITS GLORIFIED STATE

After this Christ said, *Behold!*

I looked and I saw the World Soul "die to itself" while being embraced by Sophia and Christ, who anointed the Earth. They beheld the Earth and all of its goodness—this precious, precious Earth.

Christ told me to look again. I looked and saw the heavens part. I saw the spiritual Hierarchies. They were holding the seed of the Earth in its glorified state. It was clear as glass, like a crystal. I could see into the Earth, and I could see all eternity within the Earth!

Then I heard the heavenly chorus. They were rejoicing: *It is fulfilled!*

The Earth was then a *Grail* for the entire Cosmos!

And we are part of that Grail!

It is our own transformation that brings about the transformation of the Earth. Each and all of us, wherever we are on our journey, are important and precious for the whole plan of evolution. We are beheld in our journey—the journey that began with the Fall and continues now through spiritual awakening, leading through death and resurrection. *This is the Holy Grail.*

After this, it was time for me to return. Many saints escorted me back into present time.

God hath purified the hem of Her purity from the knowledge of the concourse of names in the realm of eternity, and Her face from the view of all who are in the kingdom of creation.

When She arose with the ornament of God from Her palace, She looked with one glance toward the sky. The people of the heavens swooned at the rays of Her visage and at the wafting of Her perfume. Then She looked with another glance toward the earth, and it was illumined by the lights of Her beauty and the loveliness of Her splendor.

Then I drew near, till She stood before my face and gave utterance as a dove warbles in the realm of eternity, as though speaking in the wondrous music that hath no words, letters or sounds. It is as though all books appeared in commentary on the songs of Her innovation.

—Baha'ul'lah

14

ETERNAL ISRAEL

As the vision began,[1] I was traveling in the spiritual world. I saw a luminous city, off in the distance. I wanted to go to it. Angelic beings were streaming in and out of the city.

I saw the being of John the Baptist, hovering above. We were outside of the gates. There was much activity happening with the angels.

John spoke to me:

> I went before you to prepare a place in the wilderness, a place of refuge. Behold the City of the Lamb and His Bride, which dwells on the shining mountain! I am calling you to witness this great City, which is prepared for those whom the Bridegroom calls. And the way by which one may enter in is through the wedding of the Lamb and His Bride within. This wedding takes place in the Holy of Holies within the human being's heart.
>
> Behold! The Bridegroom is beckoning to all from His great City. And His City is the bridal chamber, and He prepares you to be His bride. He is coming for you. And He shall wed Himself to you. He loves every human soul and wishes to unite Himself with all.

I saw the Bridegroom! He was so beautiful! He spoke to me:

> You beheld the first coming of the Son of God. My first coming is encrypted in your being—all the gestures and the words

---

1   June 15, 2012.

of My first coming. You beheld My deeds and My sacred, holy gestures. It is all within you. O, beloved!

And now, behold My second coming. There is a gospel of My second coming. This gospel includes and encompasses the gospel of My first coming. And you shall record it—the gospel of My second coming—both in your heart and soul, and by the words that you shall write. You shall bring the gospel of the first coming and the second coming together. For My gospel is one eternal round, and is always proceeding from the realm of the Father. My Word emanates from the Father's kingdom. And My Word is eternal. And I ask you to bear My Word.

And there are gestures for My second coming, which have been given to you through My servant, who communes with Me in the starry realm. I call specially prepared human beings to bring forth these gestures. This began at the onset of My second coming, and is now being given in a way where this can go forth to be received by those who are ready to receive.

It is by these gestures that I may enter through the gates of those hearts who are ready to receive Me. For they bring Me to you. And the space is prepared for Me to dwell in you. This is being done through the will. The gestures purify the will. And I am the purifier of the will. I purified the will in My first coming through My deeds, through My sacrifice on Golgotha. For I gave My will over to the will of the Father. I am the only one who has done this completely. And it was not done without unfathomable suffering and ineffable laboring.

To enter into My great City, the will must be purified. It is only by will that has been transformed into love that one may travel into My city and enter in by the gates and pass through the sentinels, who stand guard. *Love purifies the will.* And I AM Divine Love.

And you may know the Love that I am by knowing My Bride, Holy Sophia, who is Wisdom.

In Her coming, Her descent, She shall make Herself known, also by certain gestures. For there are gestures of the Lamb and gestures of the Bride. And there are gestures that are sacred to their marriage union.

And certain souls are being prepared through the Holy Soul to welcome those gestures that can be given to prepare for Sophia's coming. For Her glorious entrance into the Sun sphere, certain souls are called to be vessels on Earth: to hold Her in prayer, by word and gesture, and to be Her pillars on Earth. The city of the Lamb and His Bride is thereby created first on Earth, etherically, through the assistance of those human beings who are in the process of becoming the tenth hierarchy.

Some of you spent time as angelic beings between lives on Earth. And you were called to incarnate again to bring the angelic together with the human in the physical realm, to do the work of angels while in human bodies. Therefore you are taught their language, so that you may remember their language. And as you show this language to others, it facilitates the transformation of human beings.

My kingdom shall come and shall reign on Earth in human hearts. And I come to claim hearts to be the building stones of My great city, which is the union of My mystical body and the mystical body of Mary Sophia. *Together we are the Heavenly Jerusalem.* And whoever partakes of My body and blood, and the mystical milk and the nectar of My Bride, becomes our body. We are the body of the church and the church is in you. You are the foundation of the church of Christ and Sophia. And it is not a church made of stone and glass. It is the church of the purified human soul. This is our body on the Earth.

Whoever partakes of our body has our Life, our Light, and our Love within them. And We are founding our city. We are founding it in the wilderness of humanity. For the human soul now finds itself in the wilderness. We call souls to come out, to come out from the dark cities. Awaken! And arise! And come to us in the wilderness.

We are preparing the way for you. And the journey is an initiation. And there are many trials. Keep your eye on us! You shall travel by love, and the sacred gestures will bring you safely to us. Whoever partakes of our body shall belong to us, with us. We will be in you, and you shall be in us. Awaken and arise and heed our call. Have courage! Have hope!

Just as the being of John the Baptist prepared the way in the first coming, and welcomed souls in the wilderness, and showed the people the Messiah, so now he is here for the second coming to help us find our way to the place that has been prepared for us in the wilderness. And this place is etheric. It is a place of safety and protection. And the gospel of the second coming comes from this place. The prayers and the gestures provide sustenance—even the breath of life—that nourishes human souls. And each soul must find its own way. The way is made known through the gospel of the second coming, along with the gestures and the prayers.

Eternal Israel is here! Eternal Israel! It is so beautiful! Christ and Sophia reign together in Eternal Israel. I see Eternal Israel. It is right here.

Lift up your hearts and souls and be glad. Eternal Israel is here. You are Her holy disciples, who carry the gospel in you, the gospel of Eternal Israel. Your heart is a book of light, and you shall go out and read it to others. You are the emissaries of Eternal Israel.

Do not fear the forces that may come up against you. The gospel, the good news of Eternal Israel, shall protect you. You are protected by the Word.

> *O Eternal Israel—*
> *You are the well of living waters that never runs dry.*
> *You are the bastion of peace.*
> *You are the temple of the human soul.*
> *You are crowned with the stars.*
> *And you crush the serpent's head.*
> *You are living and breathing and moving in us.*
> *You exist for all eternity—O Eternal Israel!*

Eternal Israel! As human will becomes purified, Your walls take form. You are built out of the forces of love that issue forth from purified human will. It is from this that the walls of the holy city shall rise up.

Eternal Israel! You behold us, You witness our strivings to better ourselves. We hunger for You, O beautiful city! For You are our homeland, and we ache to come to You and be succored by You and comforted in our travails. Give us the strength and courage in community to turn away from the darkness that keeps us from knowing You.

As we join together in community, may we—together—purify ourselves. May our eyes be open, and may our ears hear Your word. For Your word shall lead us until we are safely home in You.

Eternal Israel shall be everything we need. All of our yearnings are met. We are nourished, comforted, and protected. She shall give to us whatever it is that we need.

Be at peace! Seek Eternal Israel in silent meditation. As your heart hungers for Eternal Israel, so shall it be fed and nourished by the Divine Love and the Eternal Word and Divine Wisdom. Therefore be at peace. Know that there is a place for you, where angels welcome you.

Amen.

Note: When I was getting ready to leave the city to come back, the angels flew me up over the city. When I was over the city, I saw that it was so ineffably beautiful! It looked like the flower of life (a sacred geometrical form) made from the wings of the angels. All of a sudden it rose up as a huge sphere, full of harmonies, right over me. It seemed to know that I could not take it in, so it retreated from my view. It knew that it could not wholly envelop me, that I would have been completely consumed by the fire of its light. The angelic beings were the domes and the spires of the temple-like structures.

O Holy Mary-Sophia, Daughter of God,
Extend to me now Thy bounteous mercy.
Envelop me in Thy loving embrace,
That I may know Thy love and the love of Thy Son.
Vanquish every foe; subdue the evil serpent.
Protect me in Thy starry mantle
And keep me in Thy Immaculate Heart
Until that day comes
When a new Heaven and a new Earth
Shall rise together in glory—
Watch over Thy handmaiden [or servant],
O Holy Mary-Sophia.
Amen.

Prayer given to Estelle Isaacson by Mary-Sophia
December 11, 2009

PART TWO

Robert Powell

THE COSMIC DIMENSION OF SOPHIA
AND THE ROSE OF THE WORLD

15

Sophia and World Evolution

Pondering the question "Who is Sophia?"—the theme of the preface to this book—raises further interesting questions of a philosophical and theological kind about the nature of the Godhead. These questions were asked by some thinkers in the ancient world, but then with the rise of Christianity the theme of Sophia more and more receded into the background. The main reason for this was that early Christians identified Sophia with Christ. With this, at one stroke Sophia disappeared from human consciousness, at least in the Christian world. Christianity, because it developed increasingly as a patriarchal religion, lost the Divine Feminine—although there was (and still is) devotion to the Virgin Mary. On the other hand, however, in the Russian Orthodox Church there lives a devotion to Sophia. It is not immediately apparent how this came about. One can see from the various Sophia icons from the Russian tradition that all of them show Sophia as a majestic divine feminine being who is raying out wisdom. Above Her is Christ, so She is clearly not the same as Christ. To Her right is the Virgin Mary, so She is clearly not the same as the Virgin Mary. To Her left is John the Baptist. This is something—the Sophia icon tradition—that has lived in the history of the Russian Church. In fact there are two cathedrals named after Sophia: the cathedral of Divine Sophia in Kiev in the Ukraine, which was founded in the eleventh century, and the cathedral of Holy Sophia in Novgorod, north-west of Moscow, also dating from the eleventh century, which was regarded for centuries as the spiritual center of Russia.

Sophia, the All-Wisdom of God
17th-century icon (The Beuroner Kunstverlag, Beuron)

Moreover, there are also numerous Sophia churches in Russia. The Russian people simply took this devotion to Sophia as a matter of fact, without really questioning it or asking: Who is Sophia? And there is even a church liturgy, going back to the seventeenth century, which is dedicated to Sophia in the old Slavic language (Church Slavonic). All this shows that in the Russian tradition there has lived an enduring devotion to Sophia.

The great Russian philosopher Vladimir Solovyov, who was born in 1853 and studied philosophy in the West, had the mission to help the Russian people in the development of philosophy. Already as a child, in the tenth year of his life, when he was attending a church service in Moscow, he had a vision of Sophia who appeared to him as a radiant divine feminine being wrapped in azure light. On this account a sense of Sophia was living in him. It was a living presence, not just something that he had merely seen from the icons. He knew that Sophia is a real being. In his philosophical quest he was searching for the deeper meaning: Who is Sophia, and what is the relationship of Sophia to the Trinity—the Father, the Son, and the Holy Spirit, who are imbued with masculine qualities?

His search led him to London. He studied in the Library of the British Museum, and there one day he had a second experience of Sophia. This time he saw only Her face. She said to him: "Go to Egypt." And that is what he did. He took the train across Europe, down through Italy, and then took the ferry from Brindisi across to Egypt and stayed at a hotel in Cairo. There were some Russian émigrés staying there. One night he received the inner message to go into the desert. He was dressed wearing a long coat, a tall silk hat, and black gloves when he set off into the desert—a very strange sight. Some Bedouin nomads captured him, uncertain whether to kill him outright or to hold him for ransom. Fortunately for him, because of his appearance they thought he was the devil, and so they released him.

That night it was approaching dawn when he had the third and most momentous experience of Divine Sophia, who appeared to him in Her full glory and showered him with love. "Today my Queen appeared to me in azure," he wrote.[1] From that point, for the rest of his life, he was devoted to helping to bring an understanding of Sophia to the Russian people. He is regarded as the founder of Sophiology—the theology of Sophia. For Sophiology, Sophia is at the pinnacle of creation. Thus all creation has a relationship to Sophia, because all of creation has come into existence by way of the Divine Wisdom that Sophia embodies. She is the "plan" of creation and also participates in the work of creation.

---

1   Allen, *Vladimir Soloviev: Russian Mystic*, p. 117.

In the Book of Proverbs, chapter 9, there is a reference to Sophia's temple having seven pillars. This gives us some idea about the nature of Sophia. To use an analogy: architects, before they set to work building a house, will draw an architectural plan and work from that. One could think, by way of analogy, of the creator as the great architect and Sophia as the plan. She embodies the plan of creation. The seven pillars in Sophia's temple indicate the seven stages of the unfolding of creation, what is referred to as the "seven days of creation."

As well as what came about in Russia through Sophia and the Russian sophiologists, our knowledge of the divine plan of the being of Sophia has been greatly enriched in the twentieth century through the work of Rudolf Steiner (1861-1925), whose central teaching is about the unfolding of creation through seven stages or "days." What Rudolf Steiner describes is of such detail that he gives us a picture going far beyond anything that anybody has ever taught before concerning the stages or "days" of creation. Through the teaching of Rudolf Steiner, an unveiling of the being of Sophia has taken place. In fact, Rudolf Steiner called his life's work "Anthroposophia"—"anthropos," from the Greek, means the human being and "Sophia" is the Greek for wisdom. "Anthroposophia" is a new revelation of the being of Divine Sophia, in which there is an understanding of Sophia as a divine feminine being.

One important aspect indicated by Rudolf Steiner is that Sophia is a cosmic being, whose nature embraces the whole cosmos. Thus, when we contemplate a map of the galaxy we gain insights into Sophia, who holds the blueprint for creation. Our Sun, and all the different stars/suns in our galaxy, have all come into existence from the galactic center at the heart of the Milky Way Galaxy. The *Timaeus* of Plato is an important source for Platonic cosmology, in which the Supracelestial or Transmundane Sun plays a role. Supracelestial means "beyond the stars" and Transmundane means "beyond the worldly level." The expressions Supracelestial Sun ("Sun beyond the stars") or Transmundane Sun ("Sun beyond the worldly level") can be truly understood only in light of Platonic cosmology, where our Sun can be thought of as a miniature copy of the Supracelestial Sun. We could also speak of the Central Sun, if we identify the Supracelestial Sun of Platonic cosmology with the galactic center. Could it be that Platonic cosmology, in referring to the Transmundane Sun, points to the heart of our galaxy, conceiving of it as a Central Sun from which everything else has proceeded?

Let us consider, as a hypothesis, that—along the lines of Platonic cosmology—there is a Central Sun at the heart of our galaxy. In this case, it is of immense power, as may be grasped by way of analogy. If one imagines the power of our Sun holding the nine planets and countless asteroids in their orbits, one will get a sense of the power and majesty of our Sun. Now, if we think of a Central Sun at the galactic center, the scope of its power is such as to hold at least one hundred billion suns (not planets!) in their orbits around it, including our Sun!

Modern astronomy postulates the existence of a "supermassive black hole" at the center of our galaxy. However, according to esoteric teaching, supported by Platonic cosmology, the galactic center is a divine center pouring out love to all the suns, all the stars in the heavens. As Dante expresses it in *The Divine Comedy*—giving a Christianized version of Platonic cosmology—in the highest heaven, the Empyrean, he beholds that all is "being turned like a wheel, all at one speed, by the Love that moves the Sun and the other stars."[2] This is what Aristotle called the "prime mover" at the heart of all existence.[3] Everything in our galaxy is moving around this great center. As expressed several thousand years ago in the *Rig Veda*, the most ancient religious text of the Hindu tradition, "We meditate upon the supreme effulgence of the

---

2   Dante, *The Divine Comedy: Paradiso*, canto 33, lines 142–145.

3   Aristotle, *Metaphysics* XII, 1072a.

Dante and Beatrice see God as a point of light surrounded by angels (illustration by Gustave Doré), canto 28. The Rose of the World, illustration by Gustave Doré to Dante's Divine Comedy: Paradiso; *Dante and Beatrice beholding the Empyrean in the form of a white rose (Empyrean derives from the Ancient Greek word pyr, meaning "fire").*

creative *Divine Sun,* that he may give impulse to our intelligence."[4] Moreover, Divine Sophia has something to do with this Divine Sun or Central Sun at the heart of our galaxy.

Let us look back to someone who had a deep relationship with Sophia: the Italian poet Dante. In Dante's vision—which he sets at Easter in the year 1300 and spent much of his life writing

---

4   *Rig Veda* III 62.10. It is likely that the expression *Divine Sun* used here in the *Rig Veda* is referring to our Sun—as, for example, in the *Gayatri mantra* addressed to the Sun god, Surya, who is referred to as "the divine ruler." It is also possible, though, that Divine Sun is used in the sense of Platonic cosmology to refer to the Supracelestial or Transmundane Sun, since the Sun in Hindu tradition is regarded as "the cosmic symbol for the Supreme...the Divine light and presence that fills all worlds" www.hinduwisdom.info/Nature_Worship5.htm).

An artistic rendering of the Milky Way Galaxy

down as *The Divine Comedy*—he beheld the highest realm. In Dante's vision of the highest heaven he calls this highest realm the Empyrean. Let us now contemplate the depiction by the French graphic artist Gustav Doré of Dante's vision of the Empyrean (see page 108), and let us then compare this with an image of our Milky Way Galaxy (see above). One can see the similarity. It appears that what Dante beheld in mystical vision has now been found seven hundred years later by modern astronomy. Dante describes in his vision the throne of God at the center and countless beings around the throne of God. According to Dante, the whole is fashioned in the form of "a snow-white rose."[5]

Those who know the mystical tradition relating to Divine Sophia will know that this image relates to Sophia, referred to as the heavenly rose or celestial rose. In contemplating an image of our galaxy, what are we actually beholding? Are we on some

5   Dante, *The Divine Comedy: Paradiso*, canto 31, line 1.

level beholding an image of Sophia in the form of a snow-white rose? *Is Sophia, as the wisdom or "plan" of creation, one and the same with what we see revealed in the structure of our galaxy?* Considering that Sophia—according to Her own words from the Book of Proverbs—has always had a relationship with our evolution "from the beginning of creation," it is reasonable to conclude that Sophia is a being of galactic dimension. At least, we can hold this possibility as a hypothesis.

One of the important things that Rudolf Steiner indicated was that the being whom we call Sophia is the same as the goddess whom the Egyptians called Isis.[6] We know of the great significance of Isis for the Egyptian culture and also of the significance of Osiris. Isis and Osiris were regarded as brother and sister and also as bride and groom. If we take this idea of Rudolf Steiner—that Sophia is the same as Isis—and work with it, then who were the Egyptians revering as Osiris? In various lectures Steiner describes that Osiris was how the Egyptian people saw Christ before His incarnation on the Earth. We could think of this as a pre-incarnatory revelation of Christ to the Egyptian people in the shape of Osiris, before Christ incarnated on the Earth. Against this background we can understand the words of St. Augustine, who said that, "For what is now called the Christian religion existed even among the ancients."[7]

If we grasp this background concerning the ancient Egyptian mystery religion of Isis and Osiris, we can begin to understand that the Egyptians were indeed "Christians before Christ." Before he came into incarnation on the Earth, they worshipped him as Osiris. Osiris and Isis have a deep relationship to each other and are the same beings whom we know as Christ and Sophia. This is addressed in the Revelation to John, the last book in the Bible, which is the revelation of the Ascended Christ to John the Beloved

---

6   Steiner, *Isis Mary Sophia: Her Mission and Ours.*

7   St. Augustine, *The Retractions* XII, 3.

Disciple on the island of Patmos. It is clear that the one who is called the "Lamb" in Revelations is Christ. That is also the name that John the Baptist gave to Christ, as indicated in John's words: "Behold the Lamb of God" (John 1:29). In the revelation to John reference is made to the "Bride of the Lamb" who is Sophia. There is a deep and profound relationship between Christ and Sophia. A mystery of the future is revealed in Revelations, where in the last two chapters the working together of the Lamb and His Bride is referred to. What is called the sacred marriage of the Lamb and His Bride (in Greek, *hieros gamos,* or "sacred marriage"), the picture is of *Sophia the Bride descending from above as the bearer of the new heaven and uniting with the Lamb, who through His sacrifice is bringing about the spiritualization and transformation of the Earth.* Through this sacred marriage the creation of a new heaven and a new Earth will arise—the Heavenly Jerusalem, the Holy City of the Lamb and His Bride—as described in the last two chapters of Revelations (chapters 21 and 22).

Already in chapter 12, mention is made of Sophia as a majestic cosmic being. She is depicted as the "woman clothed with the Sun, with the Moon under Her feet, and on Her head a crown of twelve stars" (Rev. 12:1). The image below is a representation of Divine Sophia based on a sketch by Rudolf Steiner that is drawn directly from chapter 12 of Revelations. He presented this sketch as the fifth of the seven apocalyptic seals.

The Russian contemporary of Rudolf Steiner (1861–1925)— Vladimir Soloviev (1853–1900)—also did much during his short life to promote consciousness of Sophia among the Russian people. His efforts gave birth to Sophiology, the theology of Sophia. There would be much to say concerning Soloviev and Sophiology, but for now let us focus on the image of the fifth seal. Let us try to understand what was at work with both Rudolf Steiner and Vladimir Soloviev. We can understand it against the background of the image of the fifth seal of the "woman clothed with the

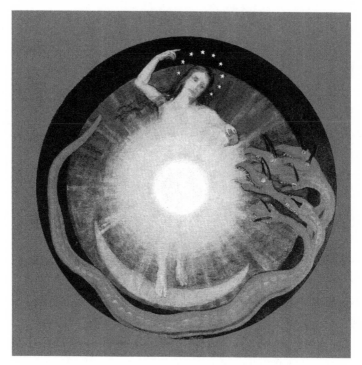

The Fifth Apocalyptic Seal by Clara Rettich
(based on a design by Rudolf Steiner)

Sun" described in Revelations. Sophia is bringing to birth a child, and—as depicted on the image of the fifth seal—She is attacked by a great red dragon with seven heads. This expresses something from metahistory to us in a remarkable way. For Vladimir Soloviev's mission was to speak to the Russian people in the name of the "folk spirit" of the Russian people, to draw the Russian people toward understanding their true mission, which has to do with Sophia.

We can understand this against the background of some remarks made by Rudolf Steiner, where he spoke of the next age, the Age of Aquarius, as the age when the Slavic peoples will come into their true mission. The Russians—and in fact all the Slavic peoples—will come into their true mission in this coming age. Their mission has to do with Sophia. That is why the image of Sophia has lived in the Russian church. The existence of the icons of Sophia in the Russian church, and also the naming of cathedrals and churches after Sophia, is not something coming from the past. It is something to do with the future. It has to do with the future mission of Russia and of the Slavic peoples. The coming Age of Aquarius will bring forth a new culture. This new culture will develop first in Russia and in the other Slavic countries and will then spread around the world to become a global culture.

If we consider this picture of the future, we can then begin to understand what took place through another Vladimir, who came after Vladimir Soloviev. That was Vladimir Lenin, who was the leader of the Bolshevik revolution, and who was instrumental in the birth of communism. Soviet communism took over not only in Russia but also in all the Slavic countries. Soviet communism represented the opposite of the coming Sophia culture. What Soloviev and many other Russians (notably Daniel Andreev, 1906–1959) were working for was to prepare Russia for the future culture of Sophia.

As John beheld in his vision on the Island of Patmos, he saw that Sophia would be attacked by a great red dragon. And what did the Bolsheviks call themselves? The Reds. The symbolism here is very transparent, if you contemplate it and see what was at work. It was literally an attack by demonic forces who worked through Lenin, and then through Stalin, after the way had been prepared by Karl Marx's *Communist Manifesto* published in 1848, shortly after the start of the "war in heaven" in 1841.[8] It is noteworthy, too, that Stalin was born in 1878—given that 1879 was the year

---

8   Steiner, *The Fall of the Spirits of Darkness*, indicates that the "war in heaven" referred to in chapter 12 of the Apocalypse lasted from 1841 to 1879. As a consequence of the triumph of the Archangel Michael, who emerged victorious in the great struggle known as the "war in heaven," the "spirits of darkness" were cast down upon the Earth—and the birth of Stalin in 1878 (and many other births around this time) can be seen in this connection.

when the war in heaven was concluded by the casting down by the Archangel Michael of the "spirits of darkness" upon the Earth. The way the dark forces work is that they see what the true image is for the future, and they substitute a caricature or an inversion of it. It is often able to take hold, because it has some element of truth.

As remarked upon already, the future age of Sophia will be an age of the flourishing of community, brotherhood and sisterhood, called in Revelations "Philadelphia." The Greek word *delphos* means "the womb," and *adelphi* means "springing from the same womb"—i.e., brothers and sisters come from the same womb. Philadelphia signifies the love that exists between brothers and sisters coming from the same womb. In a more extended sense, Philadelphia is the community of brotherly and sisterly love. The longing for community was the seduction that lay at the root of Soviet communism. Communism is supposedly based on community. But as the world then witnessed, it turned out to be a dictatorship of an élite, who led their extravagant lifestyles at the expense of millions of people whom they subjected to their will. The element of truth in communism was the longing of the Slavic people for community. This was the lure, the promise of community. However, what took place did not lead to a community of free spirits, but rather to the subjugation of the people to the will first of an elite group and then of a cruel dictator. The great tragedy that overcame Russia and the Slavic peoples was the preempting by dark forces of the future that is to arise in the coming Age of Aquarius. The visions presented in Revelations are true. They offer a picturing of the future, but we have to learn to read them properly, and this is what is meant by "reading the images of the Apocalypse"—this being something that we need to learn in order to understand on a deeper level the spiritual background to what is taking place in the world at the present time.

At the time of John, of course, all of this with regard to Soviet communism was far in the future, but for us now it lies in the past.

During the time of Soviet communism the vision of the true future of Russia was kept alive in at least one person, Daniel Andreev, who has been called the "Russian Dante." The great work of Daniel Andreev—*The Rose of the World*—is very important as a continuation of what emerged with Vladimir Soloviev as the stream of Russian spirituality devoted to Divine Sophia. Rosa Mira is the Russian title; *The Rose of the World* is the English translation of this title. It is a difficult book to read, because Daniel Andreev was faithful to everything that was communicated spiritually to him. It was said in a language that is not really known. He uses many expressions that are unknown in any language. However, he does give a glossary to explain what these expressions mean; but when one is reading the book it is very challenging because of expressions like *Shadanakar, Bayushmi,* and *Zatomis.* However, if one perseveres, an extraordinary revelation is presented in this work. But there are also definite errors in this book. Perhaps these have arisen in translation. Nevertheless, the general message of the book is very inspiring because it is all about the coming of Sophia—this being central to the arising of the Rose of the World as the coming world culture of the Age of Aquarius.

Through my own research I have been able to confirm Daniel Andreev's basic thesis of the future incarnation of Sophia. Concerning this, we are approaching an event comparable to the incarnation of Christ two thousand years ago. This event will have an enormous impact on the whole planet. We can contemplate this coming incarnation of Divine Sophia with the help of star wisdom (Astro-Sophia). Through the wisdom of the stars, it is possible to penetrate to an understanding of the coming incarnation of Sophia, which culminates during the coming Age of Aquarius. In the next two chapters of this book, I have written about the stages of Sophia's descent leading to the creation of the Rose of the World.

16

STAGES OF THE DESCENT OF SOPHIA

To gain an initial overview, let us hold in consciousness that the stages of incarnation of Sophia are the same as those of the incarnation of Christ, the Logos. Therefore, let us follow the stages of this incarnation of the Logos, starting with the Central Sun at the heart of our galaxy as the place of origin of Christ and Sophia, who each follow the same path of incarnation. In the case of Christ, His descent from the Central Sun began long ago and took place in stages. An important stage was the entrance of Christ into our local part of the galaxy, the Orion Arm, located between the Sagittarius Arm and the Perseus Arm—two of the great spiral arms extending out from the galactic center, as can be seen in the map of the Milky Way Galaxy. From this map it can be seen that there are four spiral arms—two major and two minor—proceeding from the center of the galaxy. There are also some side arms, one of these being the Orion Arm. Our Sun is located on the inside of the Orion Arm, looking toward the galactic center in the direction of Sagittarius—hence the name *Sagittarius Arm.*

Many thousands of years ago, Christ descended from the local part of our galaxy to unite with our Sun. After entering our solar system, the fact of His having united with the Sun was proclaimed about 6000 BC by Zarathustra, the founder of the ancient Persian religion of Zoroastrianism. Just as the ancient Egyptians had their own name, Osiris, for Christ in His pre-incarnatory form, so Zarathustra gave the Persian name *Ahura Mazda* to the being whom he beheld united with the Sun—the One to whom we now

A new map of the Milky Way Galaxy
(John Roach for National Geographic News, *June 3, 2008)*

refer as Christ. Then for humanity and the Earth the most important stage occurred about two thousand years ago, when Christ
descended from the celestial realm of the Sun into the human being
Jesus of Nazareth at the moment of the baptism in the River Jordan.
This is the moment that is addressed in the words: "This is my
beloved Son, whom today I have begotten" (Luke 3:22). This is how
it is expressed in the Codex Bezae.[1] In most other manuscripts of
the Luke Gospel, one reads: "This is my beloved Son, in whom I
am well pleased." However, with this version—see also Matthew

1   This is the wording of the manuscript of the Luke Gospel known as
    Codex Bezae from the fifth century. This wording is supported when one
    compares with other comparable texts—for example, Psalms 2:7, "The
    Lord said to me: 'You are my son. Today I have begotten you.'" Another
    comparable text is that of Hebrews 5:5, "So also Christ did not exalt
    himself to be made a high priest, but was appointed by him who said to
    him, 'You are my Son, today I have begotten you.'"

3:17—the significance of the moment of the incarnation is not brought out as it is in the Codex Bezae manuscript of the Gospel of Luke, where one reads: "This is my beloved Son, whom today I have begotten." This moment of baptism in the Jordan signified the incarnation of the Logos into the human being Jesus of Nazareth. It denoted the beginning of the divine mission of the God-Man, Christ Jesus, which lasted for 3½ years. I was able to scientifically exactly date most of the major events in the life of Christ as described in *Chronicle of the Living Christ*.[2] It emerges that Christ's mission was to bring the impulse of divine love from the Central Sun (Plato's *Supracelestial Sun*) for the Earth and the evolution of humanity.

There was some knowledge of this in early Christianity, when Christ was referred to as the *Spirit of the Sun*. Underlying this appellation was a knowledge that Christ came from a higher world as a cosmic being—from the Sun—and perhaps with this appellation there was even an intuitive sense on the part of some that, ultimately, Christ originated from the Central Sun, the Supracelestial Sun of Platonic cosmology, from which all stars, including our Sun, have been born.[3] This intuitive sense is implicit in a deeper understanding of Christ's words: "I and the Father are one" (John 10:30).

Similarly, speaking of Sophia as the "woman clothed with the Sun," She is also an emissary from the Central Sun as the bearer of the divine feminine aspect of the Godhead and is referred to

---

2   Powell, *Chronicle of the Living Christ.*

3   It lies beyond the scope of this book on Divine Sophia to enter into the complexities of cosmogony concerning the coming into being of the universe and, in particular, our galaxy. While the vast majority of stars (Suns) in the Milky Way Galaxy have been born from the Central Sun at the heart of our galaxy, there are also second generation stars that have not been born directly from the galactic center—for example, the "baby stars" within the Orion nebula, a star-formation region at the heart of our local part of the galaxy, the Orion Arm. Second generation stars are born by way of star formation, a process by which dense regions within molecular clouds in interstellar space—"stellar nurseries" or "star-forming regions"—collapse to form stars. Second generation stars are thus the offspring of first generation stars that have been born directly from the galactic center.

in the Book of Revelations as the *Bride of the Lamb*.[4] In the case of Christ and Sophia, we can speak of *God-born* beings coming directly from the heart of God at the center of our galaxy—Christ representing the divine masculine and Sophia the divine feminine. *God-born beings* have to be distinguished from all other beings, who are *created beings*. Angels, and all beings of the celestial hierarchies, and also human beings and all other beings are created beings. However, Christ and Sophia are God-born beings. This means that they are essentially and substantially part of the Godhead, the Divine Heart at the center of our galaxy. (There is a manifestation of the Creator's Divine Heart in the form of a Central Sun at the center of every galaxy, whereby the Godhead is mystically present throughout the universe.) When Christ spoke the words: "I and the Father are one" (John 10:30), what is meant by this? To understand the cosmic being of Christ, one has to grasp that the essence of His being extends all the way to the Central Sun, and thus He could speak these words in their full and profound sense. The same applies to Sophia, the Bride of the Lamb, who is the feminine counterpart of Christ.

To summarize: this chapter offers some background to lay the foundations for a deeper understanding as to who Sophia is. The next step is to endeavor to grasp the fact that, just as Christ incarnated upon the Earth some two thousand years ago, so also an incarnation of Sophia is underway—not an incarnation physically into a specific human being, but an incarnation into the biosphere or *life body* of our planet Earth, as the bearer of a new world culture known as the *Rose of the World*.

---

4   Concerning the Divine Feminine, see Powell, *The Sophia Teachings: The Emergence of the Divine Feminine in Our Time* and *The Most Holy Trinosophia and the New Revelation of the Divine Feminine*.

Stages of the Incarnation of Sophia
leading to the Rose of the World

Let us now endeavor to follow the stages of Sophia's incarnation. At the time when Dante wrote *The Divine Comedy* and had his vision and saw the snow-white rose, the celestial image of Divine Sophia united with the *throne of God* in the Empyrean, the highest divine realm. At the time when Dante had this vision, Sophia was still united with the Central Sun. She was at that time still dwelling in this highest sphere, the Empyrean, the divine realm united with the throne of God—the throne of God being the biblical expression employed by Dante with reference to the Divine Heart of the galaxy, from whence the creation of the galaxy proceeded. Through the star wisdom of Astro-Sophia it is revealed that since approximately 1775, Divine Sophia has become connected with the local part of our galaxy, the Orion Arm, and is now working especially through the twelve constellations of the zodiac. This is revealed in the image of Sophia crowned by twelve stars. *Sophia is clothed with the zodiac. She is at the present time working from the level of the zodiac.*[1]

Daniel Andreev's indication regarding the descent of Sophia, referred to earlier, points to "the turn of the nineteenth century," i.e., around 1800, so the date 1775 found through astrosophical research is close to this. This point in time of Sophia's entrance into the local part of our galaxy coincides with the founding of the United States of America in 1776. There is a very deep connection here between these two events, although it is not possible to go into much detail about the phenomenon here, because of its complexity.[2]

---

1   As indicated later, the date 1775 lies six hundred years before the start of the Age of Aquarius in 2375—the 600-year rhythm being that of a *cultural wave* (see Powell and Isaacson, *Gautama Buddha's Successor*).

2   See Powell, "The Guiding Spirit of America," in: *Starlight*, vol. 13, no. 2 (Advent 2013), available as a free download from www.sophiafoundation .org > newsletter. *Starlight* is the newsletter of the Sophia Foundation. It comes out twice a year.

> The goddess comes, she moves divinely fair,
> Olive and laurel binds her golden hair;
> Whenever shines this native of the skies,
> Unnumber'd charms and recent graces rise.

Briefly, in October 1775, Phillis Wheatley sent her poem about the goddess Columbia to George Washington. Her poem began by giving the guiding spirit of America the appellation *Columbia*. The later choice of "Hail, Columbia," written in 1798, as the original national anthem of the United States of America, shows the essential agreement of the Founding Fathers with what is expressed in Phillis Wheatley's poem. The very name of the capital of America—Washington, the District of Columbia—links Columbia and her champion, George Washington, for all the world to see. The goddess Columbia was deemed appropriate by the Founding Fathers of the United States to represent America. Standing for Liberty, Justice, and Peace, she appears with hindsight to have been a reflection of Sophia, mirroring certain aspects of Sophia on earth. Against this background it emerges that there is a relationship between the founding of the United States of America—noting that the Declaration of Independence took place in 1776—and the descent of Sophia to unite with our cosmos (by which is meant the local part of the galaxy, the Orion Arm) around the year 1775. Since that time Sophia has been working from the level of the zodiac, whereby the twelve zodiacal constellations represent for our solar system the *heart meridian* within the starry region of the Orion Arm.

In November 1875, one hundred years after the cosmic event of 1775, the Theosophical Society was founded in New York.[3] Theosophy, or *Theo-Sophia,* the wisdom of God, was born into cultural life at that time through H. P. Blavatsky (1831–1891), who was the central figure in the founding. Shortly before the founding

---

3   One hundred years is an important cosmic rhythm, since it is three times 33⅓ years, which is the length of the life of Christ Jesus (see Powell, *Chronicle of the Living Christ,* afterword).

of the Theosophical Society took place, the 22-year-old Russian philosopher, Vladimir Soloviev (1853–1900), while studying at the library of the British Museum in London, had a profound mystical experience of Divine Sophia one September afternoon in the year 1875. This was his second mystical experience of Sophia. Recalling his first meeting with Her at the age of nine, during the Ascension Day church service in Moscow in 1862, he inwardly asked the question: "Why have you not appeared to me since childhood?" He writes further, "Hardly had I thought these words, when suddenly all was filled with golden azure, and you were there in heavenly radiance..."[4]

Soloviev dedicated his life to serving Divine Sophia. And through him, Russian Sophiology—the theology of Sophia—was born.[5] Around the time of Soloviev's death in the year 1900, Rudolf Steiner began his lecturing activity that led to the birth of Anthroposophy (Anthropo-Sophia), the wisdom of the human being—or the wisdom that is now becoming accessible to the human being through the descent of Sophia from cosmic heights. Anthroposophy was born into the world through the Austrian philosopher and universal genius Rudolf Steiner (1861-1925). Initially active within the Theosophical Society as the initiator of the German Section of the Theosophical Society, his different approach to spirituality from that of the leaders of the Theosophical Society led to virtually the entire German Section reconstituting themselves as the Anthroposophical Society in Germany, the founding meeting of which took place on February 3, 1913. On that occasion Rudolf Steiner held a lecture titled "The Being of Anthroposophy," toward the end of which he speaks these words: "Sophia becomes the being who directly enlightens human beings. After Sophia has entered human beings, She must take their essence, their essential

---

4   Allen, *Vladimir Soloviev: Russian Mystic*, p. 111.

5   See Schipflinger, *Sophia–Maria*, chapter 15: "Sophia According to the Russian Sophiologists."

being with Her, and present it to them outwardly, objectively.... Sophia will become objective again, and She will take with Her what humanity is, and objectively present Herself in this form. Thus, She will present Herself not only as Sophia, but also as *Anthroposophia*—as the Sophia who, after passing through the human soul, through the very essence of the human being, henceforth bears that essence within Her..."[6]

These spiritual streams—Theosophy, Russian Sophiology, Anthroposophy—have arisen directly in the wake of the approach of Sophia, who around 1775 came from the Central Sun into the Orion Arm of the Milky Way Galaxy, our local part of the galaxy, for which the Greeks used the designation *cosmos*. The coming of Sophia was revealed to John on the island of Patmos over 1900 years ago when the Ascended Christ showed him the unfolding of the future of evolution. In the middle of this unfolding, recounted in the series of visions that he received and wrote down in Revelations, he suddenly beheld Sophia. John was seeing into the future. He was seeing a certain moment in time. He saw that Divine Sophia was going to appear on the world stage. He beheld Her as the "woman clothed with the Sun, with the Moon under Her feet, and on Her head a crown of twelve stars" (Rev. 12:1).

We can ask the question: When was this, or is it still to come in the future? The answer is that the appearance of Sophia onto the world stage is happening in stages, which are indicated in John's vision. The first stage has to do with Sophia coming into our cosmos, represented by the realm of the zodiac; this is symbolized by the twelve stars around Her head. The second stage has to do with Sophia coming into our solar system and connecting with the Sun. This is why John saw Her in vision "clothed with the Sun." In the third stage he beheld Her with the Moon under Her

---

6   Steiner, "The Being of Anthroposophy," lecture of Feb. 3, 1913, given at the First General Meeting of the Anthroposophical Society at Berlin. This translation by Christopher Bamford is included in *The Effects of Esoteric Development*, pp. 13–16.

feet. And then follows the fourth stage, which I will discuss below. What we are presented with in Revelations chapter 12 is a blueprint of the incarnation of Sophia. What, then, is the next stage of Sophia's incarnation, when She will come down from the level of the zodiac comprising the twelve zodiacal constellations?

According to astrosophical research, this will be around the year 2375. Astrosophy or Astro-Sophia ("Star Wisdom") is another Sophia-inspired impulse arising in our time through the advent of Sophia in our cosmos, our local part of the galaxy, the Orion Arm. Around the year 2375 Sophia will come into our solar system and unite with our Sun. Then She really will be the "woman clothed with the Sun." This will take place at an interval of about 600 years after Her entrance into our cosmos (Orion Arm) with its central band of stars—the twelve constellations of the zodiac. Advancing 600 years from 1775, we can reckon that this will occur around the year 2375, which is the date when the vernal point will enter the sign of Aquarius. Right now the vernal point is at 5 degrees in the sign of Pisces. It moves back one degree every 72 years. We can calculate the exact date when the vernal point will enter into the sign of Aquarius, signifying the beginning of the Age of Aquarius. This will be in the year 2375. This is the date that I have arrived at, based on an exact definition of the zodiac as presented in my PhD thesis *History of the Zodiac*. This date is also confirmed by a publication called the *American Sidereal Ephemeris*.[7] There the date for the beginning of the Age of Aquarius is given as 2376—a slight difference of only one year. Whichever date one takes, the beginning of the Age of Aquarius is around this time. This will be the time when Sophia will enter into the next stage of Her incarnation, approaching the Earth in accordance with the great vision that John had on Patmos over nineteen hundred years ago. She will then be literally the "woman clothed with the Sun."

---

7   Michelsen, *The American Sidereal Ephemeris*, introduction.

Preparation for the incarnation of Sophia on the Sun is already taking place. This is one of the great events in the history of our solar system. The entrance of Sophia into our solar system will signify a profound shift in our evolution, when this being of sublime majesty, beauty, celestial power, grace, and divine light and love will unite with the Sun at the start of the Age of Aquarius. Even now Sophia's influence, which at the present time (last part of the Age of Pisces) is streaming in from the world of the fixed stars, is already beginning to be received by our solar system. In the words of Daniel Andreev, this is giving rise to a new culture here on the Earth, the Sophia culture known as the Rose of the World. The more that human beings experience this inflowing of Sophia (now from the fixed stars, especially from the twelve constellations of the zodiac, but soon—in the Age of Aquarius—directly from the Sun), the more will there arise a new sense for life here on earth. A quote from Daniel Andreev's book *The Rose of the World* illustrates this:

> A mysterious event is taking place in contemporary times: new divine creative energy is emanating into our cosmos. Since ancient times, the loftiest hearts and minds have anticipated this event that is now taking place. This is an event so important that it can be compared only to the incarnation of the Logos nineteen hundred years ago. Vladimir Soloviev was given a glimpse of her when on a starry night in the Egyptian desert he experienced a stunning breach of his consciousness and saw the great feminine being with his own eyes. We call her *Zventa Sventana*, the Holiest of the Holy, She who is the brightest and all good, the experience of the feminine hypostasis of the Trinity. The long-awaited day approaches when she will descend. There she will be born in a body of enlightened ether. A host of the loftiest souls will descend with her. There she is, our hope and joy, light and divine beauty. With her coming, there will be the founding of the Rose of the World.[8]

8   Andreev, *The Rose of the World*, pp. 356–357.

This is the expression that Daniel Andreev uses for the new culture that will arise through the coming of Sophia, the Rose of the World. And this term is highly appropriate in view of Dante's great vision of Sophia in the form of a snow-white rose in the highest celestial realm, the Empyrean. The work of Sophia in our time is dedicated to helping to prepare the way for this future culture of the Rose of the World. In his visions, Daniel Andreev also points to forces of opposition to this arising of the Rose of the World in the future. The greatest opposition is presented by the incarnation of the Antichrist. The culture that will arise through the coming of the Antichrist is the opposite of what is to come into the world through the coming of Sophia and the founding of the Rose of the World. There are challenges to be faced. In meeting these challenges, we can especially find strength by focusing upon the Rose of the World and gaining an idea of the coming great culture of Sophia. Again quoting from The Rose of the World, Andreev says: "By warning about the coming Antichrist, by pointing him out and unmasking him when he appears, and also by cultivating unshakable faith within human hearts, and also by grasping the spiritual perspectives of evolution, we will help Sophia bring to birth the new culture of love and wisdom." It has to be recalled, however, that Daniel Andreev, using his own special language, does not speak of Sophia. Rather, he speaks of *Zventa Sventana*, the Holiest of the Holy. Further, it has to be clarified that when Daniel Andreev speaks of an incarnation of Sophia, he makes it clear that this is not an incarnation into a physical human being, as was the case with the incarnation of Christ in the physical human being Jesus of Nazareth. Rather, it will be an incarnation of Sophia in an "ethereal body." This ethereal body, according to Andreev, is already being prepared, and it is a body of life forces, a radiant body.

This, then, is the fourth stage of incarnation of this great being, who will work here on the Earth in a radiant ethereal body. She will bring about a far-reaching transformation, giving rise to the culture of the Rose of the World—which Rudolf Steiner calls the sixth cultural epoch, the future Slavic culture. What Rudolf Steiner describes about this future culture is elaborated upon by Daniel Andreev in his book *The Rose of the World*. It is through Rudolf Steiner that we know the exact date as to when this sixth culture will arise—starting in 3575 and extending over 2,160 years to 5735.[9] It will be the time of Sophia's incarnation in her ethereal body. This is the fourth stage—from the year 3575—after the three stages depicted in the vision of Sophia from the Apocalypse. The first stage is that of the stars ("crowned with twelve stars"— zodiacal level, 1775–2375); then will come the stage of Sophia's incarnation upon the Sun ("clothed with the Sun"—Sun level, 2375–2975); following that will be the stage of Sophia's working from the Sun through the phases of the Moon ("the Moon under her feet"—Moon level, 2975–3575). The rhythm of Sophia's incarnation follows a 600-year rhythm, which is connected with the planet Venus.[10] This is also referred to by Rudolf Steiner, who speaks of the 600-year rhythm as an important rhythm of cultural history, referring to it as a cultural wave.[11]

To summarize the stages of Sophia's incarnation, which are important to hold in consciousness: The first stage was around 1775 coming from the galaxy into our cosmos, uniting with the Orion Arm, represented by the central band of stars, the twelve constellations of the zodiac, the "twelve stars." Six hundred years later, in 2375, the Age of Aquarius will begin and Sophia will unite with the Sun, when She will appear as "the woman clothed with the Sun." A further six hundred years later, in 2975, Sophia will start to work increasingly from the Sun down to the level of

---

9   Powell, *Hermetic Astrology,* vol. 1, chapter 3 describes the sequence of zodiacal ages and corresponding cultural epochs, each 2,160 years long.

10 Ibid.

11 Steiner, *Background to the Gospel of St. Mark,* p. 153. See also, Powell and Isaacson, *Gautama Buddha's Successor: A Force for Good in Our Time,* concerning the start of a new 600-year cultural wave in 2014.

the Moon. Then the third aspect beheld in John's great vision, with the Moon "beneath her feet," will be actualized. Sophia's incarnation means that She is working ever closer toward the Earth. And then a further 600 years later, in 3575, the incarnation of Sophia in an ethereal form in a life body in the Earth's aura will take place, in what is called the "world of the elements." This is the date—the actual date is 3574—indicated by Rudolf Steiner for the beginning of the sixth cultural epoch. This is what Daniel Andreev is referring to with the birth of the Rose of the World as a new world culture inspired by Divine Sophia. Thus, with the help of star wisdom, it is possible to come to a precise understanding of the incarnation of Divine Sophia bringing the future culture known as the Rose of the World, underlying the sixth cultural epoch, which will last for 2,160 years, from 3574 to 5734. The coming down of Sophia from celestial heights is our hope, our joy, and our source of comfort for the future.

The descent of Heavenly Sophia, the feminine aspect of Christ, is mysteriously aligned with His descent at the time of His Second Coming. Christ, according to Rudolf Steiner, began to appear in the Earth's auric field around the 1930s.[12] This appearance is not in a physical body as was the case two thousand years ago, but is in the sphere that surrounds the Earth, just outside the boundaries of the sense perceptible world—in the biosphere, the body of life forces encircling the physical Earth.

The advent of Christ in the 1930s, His Second Coming, marks the onset of the greatest imaginable blessing for humankind and the Earth. However, because of the all-pervasive influence of materialism occasioned by the triumphant march of science and technology in our time, there is a widespread lack of conscious-ness with regard to awakening to the new *Presence* of Christ in the Earth's etheric aura. The Greek expression used in the Bible for the Second Coming is *Parousia*, meaning *Presence*. Thus,

---

12 Powell, *The Christ Mystery: Reflections on the Second Coming.*

although Christ through His Second Coming is ushering in a New Age—indeed, the New Age *is* the Age of Christ's Second Coming[13]—because of the general lack of awareness on the one hand of Christ's Presence and on the other hand of Sophia's inspiration from heavenly heights, there is correspondingly a vacuum present in human consciousness into which the powers of evil may work.

Looking back to the devastating events of the twentieth century—continuing in the twenty-first century—it is evident that this is exactly what occurred and is still happening. That is, it is clear that the forces of evil were able to break through and wreak havoc and destruction, clouding the dawning of the New Age not only during the first twelve years (a Jupiter cycle, 1933–1945) of the Second Coming, which began in 1933, but also since then in a more or less continuous onslaught that can be followed in relation to the 12-year rhythm of Jupiter.[14] It is noticeable that it is precisely during times when significant spiritual events are occurring, that the forces of evil choose to launch their attacks. Exactly when the onset of Christ's Second Coming began, Hitler came to power in January 1933, and the Nazi scourge that ensued was a manifestation of the work of the anti-forces, just as Stalin's reign of

---

13 Rudolf Steiner gave a very specific meaning to the term *New Age,* which is discussed at length in Powell and Dann, *Christ and the Maya Calendar,* chapter 6, and in Powell, *The Christ Mystery: Reflections on the Second Coming,* pp. 26–27, 87–90. It is evident that the New Age, also known as the *Age of Light,* is the Age of Christ's Second Coming, which began in the twentieth century and extends for some 2,500 years until the coming of the Maitreya Buddha/Kalki Avatar in the middle of the fifth millennium, shortly before the end of the Age of Aquarius (see Powell and Isaacson, *Gautama Buddha's Successor: A Force for Good in Our Time*). The New Age can be divided into two parts: the first encompasses the last phase of the Age of Pisces (ending in 2375), and the second encompasses almost the whole of the Age of Aquarius (2375–4535), whereby the first part is preparatory, comprising the work of Christ leading us into the Age of Aquarius.

14 Powell, "Sub-Nature and the Second Coming," in *The Inner Life of the Earth.*

terror in Russia was also.[15] These forces were acting in an inverted manner, as described in the vision of St. John in the Apocalypse, chapter 12. Here the manifestation of the demonic power of the dragon, who seeks to destroy the woman (Sophia), was set loose in an unprecedented way upon the Earth in Nazi Germany and communist Russia, causing widespread death and destruction and immense suffering for countless millions of people.

Through the awakening of consciousness, however, there need no longer be a vacuum into which evil is able to strike. Now (2014), eighty-one years have passed since the time of the onset of Christ's Second Coming in 1933. This is almost a complete Uranus cycle of eighty-four years. Uranus is currently (2014) in the constellation of Pisces, where it was located during the early 1930s—until April 1933. Consciousness is called to awaken so that the misery caused at the early beginning of Christ's appearance not be repeated. We are summoned to embrace Sophia's culture—her heavenly Rose of the World—at this time when Sophia is calling together communities seeking her Light.

> "Woe to you, O earth and sea, for the devil has come down to you in great wrath, because he knows that his time is short!" And when the dragon saw that he had been thrown down to the earth, he pursued the woman who had borne the male child." (Rev. 12:12–13)

In this great vision, St. John, who was gifted with a power of clairvoyance that penetrated into the far-distant future, beheld

---

15 The reign of terror began around 1929 to 1933 with the cold-blooded plan to eliminate the "kulaks" (i.e., independent peasant farmers with a couple of cows or five or six more acres than their neighbors). In Dec. 1929, Stalin announced a resolute offensive against the kulaks to break their resistance and eliminate them as a class. On Jan. 30, 1930, the Politburo approved the liquidation of kulaks as a class, decreeing that they be sent to concentration camps or banished to remote parts of the USSR. Then followed the great purge that lasted until 1939, when Stalin instituted a campaign against "alleged enemies" within his regime. Hundreds of thousands were executed, having been convicted of plotting to overthrow the government and Stalin.

clairvoyantly, whilst on the island of Patmos, the onslaught of the dragon that would take place at the time of the Second Coming. He saw in vision the birth of the Risen One taking place out of—or with the help of—the cosmic wisdom (as an aspect of Sophia), and how the powers of evil would launch an attack against the woman and her child. The Nazi scourge and the Stalinist reign of terror were manifestations of these evil powers. Hitler's expansionism, motivated by his will-to-power, resulted in his gaining control of much of Europe before the Nazi scourge was finally overcome in 1945, twelve years after the onset of Christ's Second Coming, His manifestation in the Earth's etheric aura that commenced in 1933.

17

THE SOPHIANIC TRINITY

As mentioned, the arising of the future world culture of Divine Sophia, the Rose of the World, points to the Aquarian Age (2375–4535) in which the new culture will begin to flourish. The existence of the Sophia tradition in Russia and the birth through Vladimir Soloviev (1853–1900) of Russian Sophiology are signs of the new culture that will blossom and flourish under the inspiration of Divine Sophia, initially in Russia and the Slavic world, but then embracing the whole world as a world culture. This points to a Christianity of the New Age, what we might call a Sophianic Christianity, that will arise and flourish in Russia and the other Slavic countries. This is the great promise for the future. We might ask: What other signs are there of a Sophianic Christianity in Russia?

One of the greatest monuments to Christianity is the great basilica of Hagia Sophia, constructed by Emperor Justinian in Constantinople. For a long time Hagia Sophia possessed the largest dome in the world, and its very name means *Holy Sophia*. Justinian was of the school that viewed Sophia as identical with the Logos, the Christ. So the Hagia Sophia in Constantinople is really a basilica dedicated to Christ as the wisdom of the world.

When Christianity spread to Russia in the year 988 CE, its orientation was not to the Roman Catholic world but to the Greek Orthodox tradition centered at Constantinople. The great temple of Holy Sophia in Constantinople also provided inspiration for the Russians, but they interpreted Sophia not as the Logos or

Christ but as Divine Sophia the feminine side of God, the feminine messenger of the Divine. Hagia Sophia was the archetype for Russian cathedrals such as the Holy Sophia cathedrals in Kiev and in Novgorod, built in the middle of the eleventh century. The very fact that the festival days of these two cathedrals are identical with the celebration of the birth of the Virgin Mary (Kiev) and of the Ascension of the Virgin Mary (Novgorod) points to this relationship with the Divine Feminine. So from the very beginning of Christianity in Russia and Ukraine, we find a true Sophianic quality entering in with the construction of these cathedrals dedicated to Holy Sophia.

Another testimony to the nature of worship and devotion to Sophia in Russia is to be found in the Russian icon tradition. In Novgorod we find the great icon of Divine Sophia, a majestic representation of Sophia as an angelic being seated upon a throne, radiating Her rays of wisdom to all humanity. To Her right is the Virgin Mary, to Her left is John the Baptist, as the two human beings closest to Divine Sophia. Above Her is the Risen Christ, and above Him the open book of the sacred word representing the Word of God. This inspiring icon of Sophia is found in different parts of Russia and is further testimony of the Russian people's dedication to Divine Sophia (see Sophia icon on page 104).

Sophia has been at the root of Russian Orthodox Christianity, even though within the Russian Church itself there was little understanding on a conscious level of the nature of Divine Sophia, until the time of the philosopher and mystic Soloviev in the nineteenth century. Before that time, what we find is an instinctive worship of Divine Sophia in the Russian Orthodox Church. However, we can be grateful to the Russian Orthodox Church for having preserved this Sophianic influence that disappeared by and large from the Western Church. The presence of the Divine Sophia in the Russian Orthodox tradition itself points to the future Sophianic culture that will emerge in Russia.

Vladimir Soloviev was the first within the Russian Orthodox tradition to reveal, on a conscious level, the mystery of Divine Sophia as the world soul, the mother, guide, and inspiration of future humanity. Following Soloviev, we find two key figures in the development of Russian Sophiology. These two are the Russian Orthodox priests, Pavel Florensky and Sergei Bulgakov.

Florensky was born in 1882 in Tiflis in Georgia and was from youth an extraordinarily gifted child. He was a brilliant mathematician, yet he became a priest. When the Bolsheviks came to power in the Soviet Union they planned to bring electricity to those vast lands, and, although he was a priest, Florensky was enlisted to help with this great project due to his mathematical abilities. He continued to wear his priestly robes and his great cross, and this, of course, was an unusual sight in the Soviet Union. He wore his priestly garb when he spoke at the Soviet Academy of Sciences in the year 1926. It was tolerated at the time but, later, Florensky was viciously attacked by Stalin. In the 1930s, he was sent to a concentration camp on the White Islands in the far north of Russia, and he was executed in 1937.

Florensky suffered an ignominious end, but now in contemporary Russia he is regarded as a hero and has even been called the "Leonardo" of Russian culture. He was a truly spiritual individual, with a brilliant mind and a heart devoted to the divine. His major work on Sophia is called *The Pillar and Foundation of Truth*. In this work he describes Sophia as the soul of the world:

> This sublime, royal and feminine nature who is not God or the eternal Son, nor an angel or one of the saints: Is she not the true synthesis of all humanity, the higher and more complete form of the world, the living soul of nature and the universe?

He continues:

> Sophia is the grand root of the synthesis of everything that is created, that is, the entire creation and not just all creatures.

Sophia is the guardian angel, the ideal person of the world, its formational foundation.

Florensky's Sophia teachings are drawn from the Russian Orthodox tradition, from the tradition of the whole Church back to its foundation, and from the Books of Wisdom from the Old Testament. Florensky tried to find a pure teaching of Sophia that would be acceptable within the Russian Orthodox Church. In this respect Florensky differs from Soloviev, who incorporated teachings of the mystics such as Jakob Böhme. Florensky focused upon a purely Christian interpretation of Sophia from the Christian tradition without including any Gnostic elements such as we find in Jakob Böhme's work. Florensky also pointed to the central significance of the Virgin Mary as a manifestation and incarnation of the Divine Sophia. Concerning the relationship between Mary and Sophia, Florensky writes:

> Sophia is the first created and the first redeemed, the heart of redeemed creation. She is the Church, that is, the whole of everyone who comes to enjoy redemption and makes up the body of Christ. Sophia is personal virginity, that is, the power which makes a human being entirely whole. Mary carries this virginal power in her par excellence. She is, therefore, the manifestation of Sophia, that is, Sophia incarnated.

Thus, although Florensky came to this perspective independently, his views concerning Mary as the incarnated Sophia are identical with the teaching of Jakob Böhme.

Florensky was a personal friend of the Russian priest Sergei Bulgakov (1871–1944), perhaps the most prodigious of the Sophianic theologians. At the time of the Bolshevik Revolution, Bulgakov was exiled from Russia and went to live in France, where he later became head of the Russian Orthodox Seminary in Paris. He dedicated his life to expounding his teachings concerning Sophia, and his works comprise the most comprehensive body of knowledge on Sophiology. Bulgakov's purpose was, as for Florensky, to present Sophia in a way that would be acceptable to his fellow priests and theologians of the Russian Orthodox Church. In this, as with Florensky, Bulgakov did not derive anything of his teaching from Gnostic sources outside of the Church, but concentrated solely upon the Church tradition. Nevertheless, in his exposition of the nature of Divine Sophia, Bulgakov later ran into conflict with the Moscow authorities and he was condemned on account of his Sophia teachings.

What was it about Bulgakov's views of Sophia that caused him to become viewed as a heretic? It was his idea that Sophia is the *ousia* (to use the Greek word), the substance that is common to the three persons of the Holy Trinity—the Father, the Son, and the Holy Spirit. This idea aroused the suspicion within Bulgakov's fellow theologians that Sophia could be put forward as a fourth hypostasis alongside the Father, the Son, and the Holy Spirit. However, let us hear what Bulgakov himself says concerning this idea of Sophia as the *ousia* or substance common to the Holy Trinity. Bulgakov wrote:

> The three divine persons of the Holy Trinity have a life in common, that is, an ousia, Sophia. However, this does not mean transforming the Trinity into a Quaternity.

Here Bulgakov denies that the idea of Sophia being the common life of the Holy Trinity would transform it into a Quaternity. Nevertheless, it was for this that he was condemned. This did not affect Bulgakov's position as the head of the Russian Orthodox Seminary in Paris. He continued to write and carry out his functions as a priest, but from this time onward his writings bore the stigma of heresy.

I was present in 1996 at a Sophia conference in Rome, to which Russian theologians as well as Roman Catholic priests and theologians had been invited. The theme of this conference was "Sophia as the Bridge between East and West." I learned that up to the present time within the Russian Orthodox Church the teachings of Bulgakov are still regarded as heretical. I also learned there is hope within the Russian Orthodox Church that there will one day be a great council dedicated to Sophia. First held by Soloviev, the dream to unite East and West still persists.

Russian Sophiology, a rich theological and philosophical tradition founded by Soloviev, and continued by Florensky and Bulgakov, suffered great setbacks under the communist regime of Stalin and awaits a full reemergence in the future.

Valentin Tomberg (1900–1973) was of central significance for the Russian Sophia tradition, and he carried it a stage further. It is my conviction that he represents the pinnacle of the Sophianic tradition in Russia up until the present time. I believe his teachings will occupy humanity for millennia, just as the teaching of the Holy Trinity within the Christian tradition has occupied theologians from the fourth century down to the present time.

What are his teachings concerning the Divine Sophia? We can enter into them if we first review Florensky's views and see how Valentin Tomberg's teachings go a stage further and completely transform them. According to Florensky, based on the Wisdom Books of the Old Testament, Sophia is a created being, the first created being. And as the first created being She is the highest created being of all existence. Being the very first created being, She came forth from the womb of the Holy Trinity, and therefore has a relationship to each member of the Holy Trinity. In the eyes of Florensky, Divine Sophia as the first created being has a relationship to the Father, the Son, and the Holy Spirit. Florensky states:

> Sophia participates in the life of the Trihypostatic Godhead. She enters into the bosom of the Trinity and she partakes of Divine Love. But, being a *fourth* created person she does not "constitute" Divine Unity, nor is "Love," but only *enters* into the communion Love *and is allowed to enter* into this

communion by the ineffable, unfathomable, unthinkable humility of God. From the point of view of the *Father*, Sophia is the ideal *substance*, the foundation of creation, the power or force of its being. If we turn to the *Son*, the Word, then Sophia is the *reason* of creation, its meaning, truth or justice. Lastly, from the point of view of the *Holy Spirit*, we find in Sophia the *spirituality* of creation, its holiness, purity and immaculateness, that is, its beauty.

Florensky here elaborates three aspects of Sophia as the first created being. The first aspect is that of Sophia as the original substance of the creation in Her relationship to the Father. Secondly, that Sophia is the wisdom of creation in relationship to the Son, to the Word. Thirdly, that Sophia is the beauty and spirituality of creation in relation to the Holy Spirit. Tomberg goes a stage further, in that he speaks of Sophia not simply as having three aspects but of Sophia as being three *persons*. He speaks of a Sophianic Trinity parallel or complementary to the Holy Trinity. In this profound teaching, the Divine Feminine is a Trinity comprising the Mother, who complements the Father, the Daughter who complements the Son, and the Holy Soul who is the counterpart of the Holy Spirit. This Divine Feminine Trinity is thus another side of the Godhead, complementary to the masculine Trinity of the Godhead of Father, Son, and Holy Spirit.

To contemplate some of the far-reaching implications of Valentin Tomberg's Sophia teachings, let us dwell for a moment on this Sophianic Trinity of Mother, Daughter, and Holy Soul. How can we conceive of this Trinity?

Astronomers nowadays consider the act of creation as occurring at a definite moment in time and speak of it as the Big Bang. I do not subscribe to the Big Bang theory, but I would say that if we go back far enough there is indeed a definite beginning to the coming into existence of creation. However, if we go back prior to this time, what would we find?

There would be the Godhead, the original Primordial Being, who is neither masculine nor feminine—the Creator, who is the Primordial Being of all existence. At the moment when the creation begins, however, we find a polarization taking place within this Primordial Being of the Godhead, a polarization into the part of the Godhead that goes into the Creation and that part of the Godhead which remains transcendental to the Creation.

In philosophical terms, we have, therefore, a transcendental aspect and an immanent aspect of the Godhead. In the light of Sophia, the transcendental aspect would be called the Father. The immanent aspect of the Godhead would be called the Mother. The word Mother itself conveys something of this. The Latin for mother is *mater* and the Latin word for matter is *materia*. We find, therefore, that the Mother can be conceived as the primordial substance of all creation. In the polarization within the Godhead at the beginning of creation, we find we can differentiate between the Creation, that is the Divine Mother, and that which is transcendental to the Creation, that is, the Divine Father.

Valentin Tomberg teaches that arising out of the primordial Godhead begotten from the Divine Father and the Divine Mother are the Divine Son and the Divine Daughter, Christ and Sophia, the Logos and Sophia. As the Word and the Wisdom of creation, the Divine Son and the Divine Daughter worked for eons of time in shaping the primordial matter of existence in order to bring forth the world as we know it, the world created through the wisdom of Sophia and the fire of the Divine Logos. According to this Sophianic perspective, therefore, we find the Son and the Daughter of the Divine who work together in the formation of the world and humanity.

And, just as we may understand that the incarnation of the Logos, Christ, took place in Jesus, so, according to Jakob Böhme and the Russian Sophiologists, there also took place an incarnation of Divine Sophia into Mary. And just as the incarnation of the Logos, the Christ, into Jesus took place at the baptism in the Jordan, so, according to Valentin Tomberg, the incarnation of Sophia into Mary took place at the event of Pentecost. Having prayed throughout the night together, the disciples gathered around Mary on Pentecost Sunday morning. On that holy day of Pentecost there took place the incarnation of Sophia into Mary, making possible the descent of the Holy Spirit, depicted as tongues of fire, above the heads of the disciples.

Having followed the unfolding of the Divine Feminine in relation to the Divine Masculine, let us consider the next stage, namely the relationship of the Holy Spirit on the one hand to the Father and to the Son, and on the other hand of the Holy Soul in relation to the Divine Mother and the Divine Daughter. In Christian theology, the Holy Spirit is conceived as weaving between the Father and the Son. The Divine Father is conceived as being at rest outside of the Creation, while the Divine Son, having incarnated into a human body upon Earth, is seen as having entered into the center, into the heart of creation. Between the Cross of Golgotha and the Father, transcendent to all creation, weaves the Holy Spirit as the one who renews and revitalizes all that is living. The Holy Spirit is conceived of as one who enlightens, leading humanity onward to ever-higher levels of spiritual consciousness.

Let us now consider the Divine Feminine Trinity of the Mother, the Daughter, and the Holy Soul. The Divine Mother is essentially the whole of creation, embracing all the stars, planets, Sun, Moon, the Earth, and all living creatures. Valentin Tomberg teaches that the heart of the Divine Mother, as we human beings living here on this planet experience Her, is to be found in the center of the Earth and that the plant kingdom resonates with the very heartbeat of the Mother. The Divine Daughter is the wisdom of the cosmos, pictured as the soul of the world embracing the entire cosmos extending from the realm of the fixed stars down to the planets and the Moon. This awe-inspiring image of Sophia as the world soul can be found in the Book of Revelation, where, as I mentioned earlier, She is depicted as a woman clothed with the Sun, with the Moon under Her feet, and upon Her head a crown of twelve stars.

Between the Divine Mother in the center of the Earth and the Divine Daughter, Sophia, as the world soul, weaves the Holy Soul, the third aspect of the Divine Feminine Trinity. The Holy Soul is the creator of community, who ensouls and elevates groups of human beings in the progress of unfolding evolution. We find an example of this in the spiritual tradition of Israel that conceives of the Shekinah as the soul of the community of Israel. Here Shekinah corresponds to the Holy Soul weaving between the Divine Daughter and the Divine Mother. In this Sophia teaching of the Divine Feminine Trinity—Mother, Daughter, and Holy Soul—we reach the pinnacle of the Sophia tradition of Russia. This central teaching of the Divine Feminine Trinity will be a source of inspiration for seekers of divine wisdom in the coming ages, just as the teaching of the Holy Trinity—Father, Son, and Holy Spirit—has been a source of inspiration for Christians in ages past. Valentin Tomberg arrived at an extraordinary understanding of the Divine Feminine synthesized in these three persons—Mother, Daughter, and Holy Soul.

18

SOPHIA AND THE NEW WORLD CULTURE:
THE ROSE OF THE WORLD

Purity, or virginity, is something that the devil (Lucifer) and satan (Ahriman) fear. Unfortunately, in our time, purity is most seriously under attack. This presence of the spiritual force of purity is at risk in the world. One can say only that Ahriman has been very successful in making sure that the one force that could really put him in place, the force of purity, is not present in the world. Consider the prevalence of child and adult pornography—not to mention violence and explicit sexuality in the media. Considerable background to this force of purity is given in the book *Meditations on the Tarot*[1] in the Arcanum called *Force* (chapter eleven), which is about the unstoppable force of purity being the one force that the opposing beings (Lucifer and Ahriman) fear. This appears to be decreed in the divine order.

I refer to this force of purity and its enemies because it is a very deep esoteric truth which is important to hold in consciousness as a signature of our time. Note that this degradation of the feminine began a long time ago. Think back to when Ptolemy (a highly influential Greek astronomer of the second century AD) changed the orientation of the Virgin in the constellation of Virgo from a standing figure to a figure that is lying down, supine. This represented a de-throning of the Virgin, and this "de-throning" is exactly what we see in the modern world.

---

1   Anonymous, *Meditations on the Tarot*.

Relentless opposing forces are at work to remove from us our sense of uprightness which is related to purity. There is something very significant connected with uprightness and being morally upright.

There was, in Egypt, a great ritual of the raising of the *djed pillar* into an upright position, which was a symbol of the resurrection of Osiris. It was celebrated at the great temple of Abydos, in Egypt, which was an important center for the worship of Osiris. The *djed pillar* is within us, as the spinal column. It is a force of resurrection that brings our spinal column into an upright position, and in this way we become aligned with the world of spirit. At Abydos it was an outer symbolic ritual having to do with the raising up of the spinal column, because the spinal column is an expression of our humanity. This is what distinguishes us from the animals, which by and large have horizontal spines. The human being's spine is raised up into the vertical dimension, and this force of uprightness, which was seen in connection with Osiris, is represented cosmically by the force that lives in the constellation of Virgo, in turn, in its higher aspect, identical with the Arcanum *Force* as described in chapter eleven of *Meditations on the Tarot.*

From indications made by Rudolf Steiner it is evident that Sophia ("Wisdom"), who spoke to the people of Israel through Solomon, was worshipped by the ancient Egyptians as Isis. He indicated that with the decline of the ancient Egyptian culture the cosmic wisdom, Isis–Sophia, became "buried" or "killed," but that now in our time She may be found again. She may be found in spiritual realms as the Cosmic Virgin, and if She is found there, She communicates to us a new wisdom of the stars. In the New Age, the age of Christ's Second Coming, Mary Sophia may be sought also here on Earth, manifesting from within the Earth's etheric aura. She may reveal Herself to human beings not only in churches and cathedrals, such as the great cathedral at Chartres, but also in the stillness of Nature, in harmonious union with Mother Earth. She manifests as the bearer of peace into our troubled civilization. And, as Rudolf Steiner describes, it is with the help of Mary Sophia that Christ in His Second Coming is able to appear in spiritual form in our time.

> It is not on account of something happening by itself from without that Christ will be able to appear again in his spiritual form in the course of the twentieth century, but rather through human beings finding the force represented by Holy Sophia. The tendency in recent times has been to lose precisely this Isis force, this Mary force, which has become stamped out through that which has arisen within the modern consciousness of humanity. And the more recent denominations have partly obliterated a perspective concerning Mary. To a certain extent this is the mystery of modern humankind, that basically Mary–Isis has been "killed," and that she must be sought again, sought in the widespread heavenly realms with the power which Christ is able to kindle within us when we devote ourselves to him in the right way.[2]

Through Sophia's in-streaming inspiration in our time, a seed impulse toward the development of a new wisdom of the stars (Astro-Sophia, "star wisdom") is arising. The increasingly widespread awakening interest in the stars can be placed in service of Sophia, who comes to meet inwardly each human being striving to bring Christ to birth within. Christ and Sophia are central to the arising of a new star wisdom; and the New Age in which we now live provides a unique opportunity for each human being to find a new relationship with these Divine Beings who are guiding humanity and the Earth toward the spiritual goals of the future.

---

2   Steiner, *Isis Mary Sophia: Her Mission and Ours*, pp. 213–214.

THE ROSE OF THE WORLD

Often the question is asked: Why is there so much evil in the world? There are many possible responses to this question. From an evolutionary standpoint it can be said that the "mission" of evil is to call forth the good. The more that darkness and evil prevail in the outer world, the more Sophia—if we open ourselves to Her—is with us as light and goodness, and the more She may be experienced in our hearts, and in our thoughts and prayers, as a real presence in daily life. The following words quoted from the Russian spiritual seer Daniel Andreev lead from the prophecy concerning the coming of Antichrist to the creation of the new world culture through Divine Sophia, as outlined in Andreev's book *The Rose of the World*. The Sophia culture of the future is one of peace and brotherhood/sisterhood. It is the answer—on the scales of spiritual evolution—to the evil of our time. Thus, for many, it is the Rose of the World that serves to set our goals and chart our courses for what is to come.

By warning about the coming Antichrist, and pointing him out and unmasking him when he appears, by cultivating unshakeable faith within human hearts and a grasp of the metahistorical perspectives and global spiritual prospects within human minds...[we help Sophia bring to birth the new culture of love and wisdom called by Daniel Andreev the Rose of the World]...[Sophia's] birth in one of the *zatomis* will be mirrored not only by the Rose of the World. Feminine power and its role in contemporary life are increasing everywhere. It is that circumstance above all that is giving rise to worldwide peace movements, an abhorrence of bloodshed, disillusion over coercive methods of change, an increase in woman's role in society proper, an ever-growing tenderness and concern for children, and a burning hunger for beauty and love. We are entering an age when the female soul will become ever purer and broader, when an ever-greater number of women will become profound inspirers, sensitive mothers, wise counselors and far-sighted leaders. It will be an age when the feminine in humanity will manifest itself with unprecedented strength, striking a perfect balance with masculine impulses. See, you who have eyes.[3]

The words quoted above are from Daniel Andreev, the great prophet of the coming Age of Sophia and the corresponding Sophia culture that he called the *Rose of the World*. (Andreev refers to Sophia in his book as *Zventa-Sventana*, meaning "Holiest of the Holy," and *zatomis* refers to a heavenly realm within the Earth's aura.) The words of this great Russian seer are prophetic words. As indicated in my book *The Most Holy Trinosophia and the New Revelation of the Divine Feminine*,[4] Andreev points to Sophia and the coming world culture, the Rose of the World, in a most inspiring way:

> There she is, our hope and joy, Light and Divine Beauty! For her birth will be mirrored in our history as something that our grandchildren and great-grandchildren will witness: the founding of the Rose of the World, its spread throughout the world, and...the assumption by the Rose of the World of supreme authority over the entire Earth.[5]

The Rose of the World is arising through the approach of Divine Sophia toward the Earth. Her approach is calling forth the following basic qualities or attributes of the new world culture that She is creating and inspiring:

1. First and foremost: inter-religion. For Sophia all true religious and spiritual traditions are different layers of spiritual reality, which She seeks to weave together as petals of the Rose of the World. Sophia is not founding a new world religion as She approaches, descending from cosmic heights, drawing ever

---

3   Andreev, *The Rose of the World*, p. 358 [words in brackets added by RP].

4   Powell, *The Most Holy Trinosophia and the New Revelation of the Divine Feminine*.

5   Andreev, *The Rose of the World*, p. 357.

closer to our solar system. On Her path of descent, approaching our planet in order to incarnate into the Earth's aura during the Age of Aquarius, She is bestowing insight concerning each religion and spiritual tradition, thus awakening inter-religiosity, signifying a heartfelt interest in religious and spiritual traditions other than one's own. This signifies the blossoming and unfolding of the petals of the Rose of the World, creating brotherhood/sisterhood between all peoples.

2. Sophia's approach toward our planet is bringing about an awakening of social conscience on a global scale, inspiring active compassion combined with unflagging practical efforts on behalf of social justice around the world.

3. Through Sophia, a framework for understanding the higher dimension of historical processes is coming about: *metahistory*, illumining the meaning of historical processes of the past, present, and future in relation to humankind's spiritual evolution. This entails glimpses into the mystical consciousness of humanity such as may be found in the Book of Revelations.

4. On the national social-political level, Sophia's inspiration is working to transform the state into a community. The *community* of Italy, the *community* of France, etc., is the ideal for the future, rather than the political entity of the state representing (or misrepresenting) the people. And on the global scale Sophia is seeking to bring about the unification of the planet as a world community through bringing the different country communities into a harmonious relationship with one another on a religious, cultural, and economic level.

5. This world community, the Rose of the World, inspired by Sophia, will seek to establish the economic well-being of every man, woman, and child on the planet, to ensure that everyone has a roof over their heads and sufficient food to live on. Here it is a matter of ensuring a decent standard of living for all peoples of the Earth.

6. A high priority of the Rose of the World will be the ennobling of education. New methods of education are being inspired by Sophia to help bring out everyone's creative talents. We must endeavor to ennoble education, so that each person's creativity can unfold.

7. Finally, Sophia is working for the transformation of the planet into a garden. In their striving to live in cooperation and harmony with Nature, human beings are to take up their responsibility for the spiritualization and redemption of Nature's various kingdoms.

Appendix: Sophia—Sources of Inspiration

Sophia, Divine Wisdom, underlies all true religion and spirituality. There are a great many sources concerning Sophia, Divine Wisdom, and in this appendix the authors offer some which have been—and continue to be—most meaningful for our journey of exploration into the Mystery of Sophia. Thereby, of course, some wonderful sources have been omitted. We trust, however, that anyone who embarks on an exploration utilizing the following sources will on the course of their journey be led to many of the other meaningful sources that are not mentioned here—see also the books referred to in the bibliography.

Important new knowledge about Sophia has been communicated in our time by Rudolf Steiner, Valentin Tomberg, and the Russian Sophiologists.

Rudolf Steiner (1861–1925) was a twentieth century spiritual teacher who expressed a profound breadth and depth of knowledge in many different fields. He synthesized his own spiritual abilities with a dedication to scientific inquiry. The resulting "science of the spirit" (Anthroposophy) brings spiritual truths to people of the modern world in a readily understandable and highly applicable form. It provides invaluable indications for the renewal of many human activities, including philosophy, science, education (the Waldorf school movement), medicine, agriculture, economics, architecture, and the arts, including the new art forms of eurythmy and speech formation. Rudolf Steiner lectured extensively throughout Europe (more than 6,000 lectures), wrote some 65 books, and founded the Anthroposophical Society in 1913.

Steiner's books that relate to Sophia include *Isis Mary Sophia: Her Mission and Ours* and *The Goddess: From Natura to the Divine Sophia* (see these books at www.SteinerBooks.org).

Valentin Tomberg (1900–1973) was born in St. Petersburg, Russia, into a Lutheran family. Already in his youth he entered upon a serious study of Christian esotericism. He was strongly influenced by the Russian Sophiologist Vladimir Soloviev, and in his early life he was also a student of Rudolf Steiner. He wrote and lectured on Spiritual Science (Anthroposophy), primarily in relation to Biblical themes. For him Anthroposophy was a bridge to the living Christ. During World War II he joined the Greek Orthodox Church and then the Roman Catholic Church, inspired by the ecumenical ideal espoused by Vladimir Soloviev of the unity of the Christian Church. For the latter part of his life he resided in England, working for the British Broadcasting Corporation (BBC), while pursuing meditation and writing. Valentin Tomberg's writings reveal an extraordinary depth of perception that cannot fail to touch the heart of the meditative reader. His later works were written in the spirit of the great Hermetic tradition of wisdom extending back to Ancient Egypt. These writings, concerning the symbolism of Christian Hermeticism as a fusion of Hermeticism with the Christian tradition, draw not only upon the wisdom of the Bible but also upon many other spiritual and mystical traditions. An important source work for Christian Hermeticism is *Meditations on the Tarot*. Valentin Tomberg is widely acknowledged not only as a leading Sophiologist (teacher concerning Sophia), but also as one of the great mystics of the twentieth century and as the primary inspirer of Christian Hermeticism. See also Valentin Tomberg, *Christ and Sophia*.

Western Sophiologists include Jacob Böhme (1575–1624) and Louis-Claude de Saint-Martin (1743–1803). See *Wisdom's Book, the Sophia Anthology* by Arthur Versluis.

Russian Sophiologists include Vladimir Soloviev (1853–1900), Pavel Florensky (1882–1937), and Sergei Bulgakov (1871–1944), who wrote *Sophia: The Wisdom of God.* See also the book *Sophia Maria* by Thomas Schipflinger. The Russian poet and mystic Daniel Andreev (1906–1959) is also an important source concerning the new revelation of Divine Sophia in his work *The Rose of the World.*

Anne Catherine Emmerich (1774–1824) was born of poor parents near Coesfeld, Germany. At an early age she was blessed with the gift of spiritual sight (clairvoyance) and lived almost constantly in inner vision of scenes of the Old and the New Testament. She became a nun at age twenty-nine. Eight years later she had become so ill as to be confined to bed. On December 29, 1812, she received the stigmata, a manifesting of the wounds suffered on the cross, the highest outward sign of inner union with Christ. Unable to assimilate any form of nourishment, for the rest of her life she was sustained almost exclusively by water and the daily Eucharist. On July 29, 1820, she began to communicate—in states of ecstasy and in the most extraordinary detail—visions she had of the day-to-day life of Christ Jesus. These revelations continued until her death and were recorded in writing by the German author Clemens Brentano.[1]

Classical Hermetic texts include the *Tabula Smaragdina* (Emerald Table), *Koré Kosmou* (the Cosmic Virgin), and other writings from the *Hermetica*—writings from the ancient Hermetic tradition generally attributed to the Egyptian sage Hermes Trismegistus (*Hermetica*, 4 volumes).

Texts belonging to the tradition of the Kabbalah include the *Zohar* ("Book of Splendor"), which is the central work in the literature of the Kabbalah. The Kabbalah encompasses the writings of the Jewish mystical tradition (see *Zohar* in the bibliography).

---

1   See Anne Catherine Emmerich's work *Visions of the Life of Christ;* and for her significance in the Sophia tradition, see Thomas Schipflinger's *Sophia Maria.*

Thomas Schipflinger's *Sophia Maria* is an excellent resource for further studies concerning Sophia in the world's great religious and spiritual traditions. Particularly significant for Sophia as Divine Wisdom are several works belonging to the Hebrew tradition, including the Psalms and the Book of Job and the so-called "Wisdom books" of the Old Testament (Proverbs, Song of Songs, Ecclesiastes, the Book of Wisdom, and the Wisdom of Sirach). The first four are associated directly or indirectly with King Solomon; and the Wisdom of Sirach, also known as Ecclesiasticus, bears strong parallels with Ecclesiastes, and is thereby also indirectly connected with Solomon.

Also purporting to originate from the Hebrew tradition is the four-volume work *The Essene Gospel of Peace* (see especially books 2 and 4), although it should be noted that much controversy surrounds question over the authenticity of this work. For a deeper understanding of Sophia, there are a number of important Gnostic texts, such as the *Pistis Sophia* and the collection gathered in the *Nag Hammadi Library,* which contains, among other books, *The Sophia of Jesus Christ* and *The Thunder, Perfect Mind.* Also important is a work that is a new translation of and an exposition on *The Gospel of Mary* from the Nag Hammadi Library— *The Gospel of Mary Magdalene,* translated into French from the Coptic with commentary by Jean-Yves Leloup; English translation from the French and notes by Joseph Rowe. Finally, among the many significant books relating to Sophia and the Divine Feminine that could be mentioned here is a classic work, *The Myth of the Goddess,* by Anne Baring and Jules Cashford, which offers a grand overview of the Divine Feminine in history, from the Paleolithic Mother Goddess to Sophia.

All spiritually inspired architecture, sculpture, art, music, poetry, dance, and drama is relevant, if we bear in mind Sophia's title from the Middle Ages as "Patroness of the Arts."

The work of this book's authors—Karen Rivers, Estelle Isaacson, and Robert Powell—is focused on Sophia, as is the work of many others connected with various Sophia communities around the world. Communities that we know of have formed in connection with this work and exist in a number of places in the United States and Canada, as well as in Australia and various European countries, and certainly elsewhere. These communities have constellated because of a heartfelt seeking among their members to know and connect with Sophia. This work of honoring Sophia is centered upon the cognition that the human being is formed through the Divine Wisdom of Sophia, and that each human being is on a journey over a long period of time together with the Earth to grow more and more into Sophia's wisdom. This Sophia work in our time seeks to be a vessel for the worldwide community of Sophia—known as the "Rose of the World"—which is due to arise in the future during the Age of Aquarius. The Rose of the World can be likened to a spiritual flower that exists on a cosmic level, where each petal is a different religion or spiritual tradition, and where the stem is the one all-pervasive divinity that nourishes all the petals—together forming a unified blossom. It is an image of the future time when the Holy Wisdom of Divine Sophia prevails and humanity knows the unique, yet unified relationship of the world religions and spiritual traditions.

To this purpose various wisdom schools offer creative study programs that are intended to help participants toward spiritual growth and coming back into resonance with the sacred matrix of creation that is an expression of Sophia. In addition to the study programs, there is often a focus upon artistic activity with a view to activating each individual's creativity, while simultaneously cultivating community with one another. Work in community with such activities as sacred drama, choral singing, and choreocosmos—cosmic and sacred dance (eurythmy)—are central to the Sophia activities of the authors of this book, who are dedicated to serving Sophia and the arising of the future Sophia culture, the Rose of the World. Through choreocosmos, for example, not only do we have a communal form of dance but also we are connecting with the cosmos through our activity. The teachings arising through this activity—inspired by Sophia—can then go out into the greater community by way of all who receive them. At this time when there is so much negativity in the world, it is important for human beings to be able to participate in something ennobling and refining.

The spiritual training thus offered through such activities deepens our understanding of the human being's relationship to the cosmos in an experiential way, and also helps to uncover the wisdom deep within each human being—a wisdom that echoes the formative patterns imprinted on creation by Sophia.

The goal is to enter into Sophia's *School of Wisdom* and to arrive at consciousness of global unity, in recognition that all humankind is one family. To reach this level of consciousness, it is important that we develop empathy with all living beings and also that we develop the faculty of intuition. Both faculties help us to come into connection with the realm of life forces, also known as the etheric realm, where unity of consciousness is a direct experience. In turn, through the etheric realm we are able to develop a sensing and a knowing of the needs of our environment, including the human beings around us. Thus we become rightly informed and we can respond wisely and responsibly.

We are living in a time when great decisions are often made without this sense of connection to the whole. Such decisions can be cold and heartless, even dangerous. The activity of choreocosmos offers an example—from among the various Sophia activities around the world—that is most helpful here, as it is an activity which strengthens the human being's connection with the etheric realm. Through becoming conscious of this connection, we become aware of how every living creature receives Unconditional

Love from the etheric life-body of the Earth and also Divine Love from our Sun and from all the stars in the heavens, which are continually streaming down the Divine Light pouring forth from the Ultimate Source of existence. The experience of Divine Light, Life, and Love brings gratitude and awakens magnanimity. In love and gratitude one can reach out to the world and truly serve the needs of one's environment. By contemplating the stars, global oneness is awakened. All cultures of the Earth are blessed by the stars, by the Sun, Moon, and planets, through which we are connected with Sophia's "body"—She who is "clothed with the Sun, with the Moon under Her feet, and on Her head a crown of twelve stars" (Rev. 12:1).

Another example of contemporary Sophia activity is that of *Sophia Grail Circles*—communities of people who join together to form vessels to serve Divine Love and Holy Wisdom in cultivating a growing awareness of the spiritual evolution of humanity and the Earth.[2] Toward this end, participants in *Sophia Grail Circles* come together consciously and purposefully to maintain the intention and vision of Sophia's Divine Plan of creation, and as a community to connect with Divine Love and Holy Wisdom through sacred celebrations. *Sophia Grail Circles* are endeavors to focus on Divine Love and Holy Wisdom as the fountain of Life at the heart of each spiritual community. In coming together, holding this vision and intention, there arises a human weaving that serves to enable the inspiration of the Holy Soul (the third person of the Sophia Trinity: Mother, Daughter, and Holy Soul—see chapter 17 of this book) to work into the hearts of each and every person in the circle and into the heart of the community.

Lastly, the arising of *Rosamira Circles*—"*Rosa Mira*" being the Russian expression for the Rose of the World—should be mentioned. The *Rosamira Circles* are communities of friends who come together monthly to celebrate the cycle of the year in

---

2   See www.sophiafoundation.org—Activities.

its spiritual depth—devoted to the spiritual unity of humankind, drawing upon spiritual teachings from the great religions and spiritual traditions of the world, and honoring the over-arching guidance of Divine Love and Holy Wisdom for humanity and the whole Earth. The four cornerstones of the solar year (the summer and winter solstices, and the vernal and autumnal equinoxes) are generally celebrated at the festivals of Advent/Christmas, Easter, Pentecost/St. John's Tide, and Michaelmas, the latter being celebrated shortly after the autumnal equinox—the traditional date of the Michaelmas festival (Sept. 29), honoring the Archangel Michael as the Guardian of Truth and Justice. The celebration of these festivals offers a community-based path that unfolds through the cycle of the year. Additional gatherings generally take place in between these four major festival celebrations, whereby an overall monthly rhythm of gatherings to celebrate the spiritual unity of humanity throughout the entire year offers a powerful support for the community. With song, dance, and story—also readings, prayer, and liturgy—spiritual community is formed with the goal of seeking to deepen the conscious unfolding of the human soul and spirit. The *Rosamira Circles* are open to all children, youth, and adults, who seek to join together in service of Divine Love and Holy Wisdom, and to walk in spiritual consciousness with open hearts toward the future.

To summarize: The door to the Aquarian Age will open in 2375. As this date is such a relatively short time ahead in our future, we can imagine it now acting as a portal, calling groups and individuals in a preparatory way toward the lofty aims of the dawning Aquarius Age during which the culture of Sophia will blossom and flourish around the world. This approaching Sophia culture is known as the Rose of the World. Thus the birth of the Aquarian Age—almost upon us—signifies the advent of the world Sophia culture, the Rose of the World, during which brotherly and sisterly love will flourish in all hearts aligned with Sophia's loving and unifying mission. The flag-bearers of this future culture are already forming and creating communities around the world in order to sow the seeds for what will then blossom.

The new paths that are unfolding can be recognized by their moral integrity, their inherent cultivation of an attitude of loving kindness, their resolute quest for truth and wisdom, and their cultural artistry, for these are all signatures of Sophia's work in the world. In addition to the new cosmic and sacred dance forms and the devotional work of Sophia-oriented prayer, meditation, and celebratory Grail and Rosamira Circles, we can imagine many other expressions of Divine Sophia flowing into the creative inspiration of hearts hearing Her call. All of these new paths will contribute to the development of future organs of cognition through which Sophia can be known by way of an inner experience within the chalice of one's own soul.

BIBLIOGRAPHY

Alighieri, Dante. *The Divine Comedy: The Inferno, The Purgatorio, and the Paradiso.* New York, NY: New American Library, 2003.

Allen, Paul M. *Vladimir Soloviev: Russian Mystic.* New York, NY: SteinerBooks, 1978.

Andreev, Daniel. *The Rose of the World.* Hudson, NY: Lindisfarne Books, 1997.

Anonymous. *Meditations on the Tarot: A Journey into Christian Hermeticism* (Tr. Robert Powell). New York: Tarcher-Penguin, 2002. The Appendix to chapter 1 contains a translation together with a commentary on the *Tabula Smaragdina*.

Augustine. *Fathers of the Church: Saint Augustine: The Retractations* (Tr. Sr. Mary Inez Bogan, PhD). Washington, DC: The Catholic University of American Press, 1968.

Aristotle. *Metaphysics.* Cambridge, MA: Loeb Classical Library/Harvard University Press, 1933.

Aurobindo. Sri. *Savitri.* Pondicherry, India: Sri Aurobindo Ashram, 1972.

Bahá'u'lláh. *The Tablet of the Houri.* http://www-personal.umich.edu /~jrcole/houri.htm (last updated 1996).

Baring, Anne, and Jules Cashford. *The Myth of the Goddess.* New York: Penguin, 1993.

Emmerich, Anne Catherine. *Visions of the Life of Christ.* Taos, NM: LogoSophia, 2014.

Essene Gospel of Peace, vols. 1 and 2. Tr. Edmund Bordeaux Szekely. Paris: International Biogenic Society, 1981.

Florensky, Pavel. *The Pillar and Ground of the Truth: An Essay in Orthodox Theodicy in Twelve Letters.* London: Princeton University Press, 2004.

The Gospel of Mary Magdalene (Tr. Jean-Yves Leloup). Inner Traditions, 2002.

Hermetica: Writings Ascribed to Hermes Trismegistus (Tr. Walter Scott). Boston, MA: Shambhala Publications, 1985—*Koré Kosmou*, pp. 457–495.

Isaacson, Estelle. *Through the Eyes of Mary Magdalene,* 2 vols. Taos, NM: LogoSophia, 2012.

Hildegarde of Bingen. *Symphonia.* Ithaca, NY: Cornell University Press, 1988.

Merton, Thomas. *Hagia Sophia*—Christopher Pramuk, *Sophia: The Hidden Christ of Thomas Merton*, with special attention to his remarkable prose poem of 1962, *Hagia Sophia* (Collegeville, MN: Liturgical Press, 2009).

Michelson, Neil. *The American Sidereal Ephemeris*. San Diego, CA: Astro Communication Services, 1981.

Parker, David C. *Codex Bezae: An Early Christian Manuscript and its Text*. New York, NY: Cambridge University Press, 1992.

Plato. *Plato's Cosmology: The Timaeus of Plato*. London: Routledge and Keagan Paul, 1966.

Powell, Robert. *Chronicle of the Living Christ: The Life and Ministry of Jesus Christ: Foundations of Cosmic Christianity*. Hudson, NY: Anthroposophic Press, 1996.

——. *Cultivating Inner Radiance and the Body of Immortality*. Great Barrington, MA: SteinerBooks, 2012.

——. *Hermetic Astrology*, vol. 1. San Rafael, CA: Sophia Foundation Press, 2006.

——. *History of the Zodiac*. San Rafael, CA: Sophia Academic Press, 2006.

——, ed. *Journal for Star Wisdom 2013*. Great Barrington, MA: SteinerBooks/Lindisfarne Books, annual.

——. "Sub-Nature and the Second Coming" in: *The Inner Life of the Earth* (ed. Paul V. O'Leary). Great Barrington, MA: SteinerBooks, 2008.

——. *The Christ Mystery: Reflections on the Second Coming*. Fair Oaks, CA: Rudolf Steiner College Press, 1999.

——. "The Guiding Spirit of America," *Starlight* vol. 13, no. 2 (Advent 2013). *Starlight* is the newsletter of the Sophia Foundation and is available in PDF format as a free download from the website: www.sophiafoundation.org—Activities.

——. *The Most Holy Trinosophia and the New Revelation of the Divine Feminine*. Great Barrington, MA: SteinerBooks, 2000.

——. *The Sophia Teachings: The Emergence of the Divine Feminine in Our Time*. Great Barrington, MA: SteinerBooks, 2001.

Powell, Robert, and Estelle Isaacson. *Gautama Buddha's Successor: A Force for Good in Our Time*. Great Barrington, MA: SteinerBooks, 2013.

Powell, Robert, and Kevin Dann. *Christ and the Maya Calendar: 2012 and the Coming of the Antichrist*. Great Barrington, MA: SteinerBooks, 2009.

Rig Veda (Tr. Wendy Doniger). New York: Penguin Classics, 2005.

Robinson, James McConkey. *The Nag Hammadi Library in English.* Boston, MA: Brill Academic Publishers, 1997.

Rumi. *Rumi: The Book of Love* (Tr. and commentary Coleman Barks). New York, NY: HarperCollins, 2003.

Sacred Books of the Hindus. Bahadurganj, Allahabad: Sudhindra Nath Vasu, at the Panini Office, 1922.

Schipflinger, Thomas. *Sophia-Maria.* York Beach, ME: Samuel Weiser, 1998.

Steiner, Rudolf. *Background to the Gospel of St. Mark.* London: Rudolf Steiner Press, 1968.

———. *The Effects of Esoteric Development.* Hudson, NY: Anthroposophic Press, 1977.

———. *The Fall of the Spirits of Darkness.* London: Rudolf Steiner Press, 1995.

———. *Isis Mary Sophia: Her Mission and Ours.* Great Barrington, MA: SteinerBooks, 2003.

Teilhard de Chardin, Pierre. *Writings in Time of War.* New York, NY: Harper and Row Publishers, 1967.

Teresa of Avila. *The Interior Castle* (Tr. and introduction Mirabai Starr). New York, NY: Riverhead Books, 2003.

Tomberg, Valentin. *Christ and Sophia: Anthroposophic Meditations on the Old Testament, New Testament, and Apocalypse.* Great Barrington, MA: SteinerBooks, 2006.

———. *Russian Spirituality and Other Essays.* San Rafael, CA: LogoSophia, 2010.

Versluis, Arthur. *Theosophia: Hidden Dimensions of Christianity.* Hudson, NY: Lindisfarne Press, 1994.

———. *Wisdom's Book: The Sophia Anthology.* St. Paul, MN: Paragon House, 2000.

Wheatley, Phyllis. *Poems on Various Subjects, Religious and Moral.* London: Printed for A. Bell, Bookseller, Aldgate, 1773.

Zohar, 5 vols. (Tr. Harry Sperling and Maurice Simon). London-Jerusalem-New York: Soncino Press, 1984.

Gautama Buddha's Successor
A Force for Good in Our Time

Robert Powell and Estelle Isaacson

The year 2014 has a special significance that is addressed in this book by Robert Powell and Estelle Isaacson. Dr. Robert Powell is a spiritual researcher who in this short work—and in many other books—brings the results of his own research investigations. Estelle Isaacson is a contemporary seer who is gifted with a remarkable ability to perceive new streams of revelation. Both have been blessed in an extraordinary way by virtue of accessing the realm wherein Christ is presently to be found.

Powell makes the critical point that the year 2014 not only denotes the beginning of a new 600-year cultural wave in history but also that there is an ancient prophecy applying to this very same year, 2014, which can be interpreted as pointing to the onset of the twenty-first-century incarnation of the Bodhisattva who will become the future Maitreya Buddha, the successor to Gautama Buddha. Powell also makes the crucial point that the Maitreya Buddha awaited in Buddhism is the same as the Kalki Avatar expected in Hinduism.

Powell's contribution serves as an introduction to Isaacson's offering, comprising a series of six visions relating to the future Maitreya Buddha. The visions are highly inspirational, communicating something of the profound spirituality, peace, radiance, and, above all, goodness of this Bodhisattva who is Gautama Buddha's successor. His title, Maitreya, means "bearer of the good," and in Isaacson's visions he emerges as a remarkable force for good in our time.

Also included in this book are two appendices: A Survey of Rudolf Steiner's Indications Concerning the Maitreya Buddha and the Kalki Avatar and Valentin Tomberg's Indications Concerning the Coming Buddha-Avatar, Maitreya-Kalki. A third appendix discusses the significance of Rudolf Steiner's Foundation Stone of Love meditation as a heralding of Christ's Second Coming.

ISBN: 9781584201618 | 158 pages | pbk | $18.00

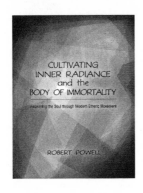

CULTIVATING INNER RADIANCE
AND THE BODY OF IMMORTALITY

AWAKENING THE SOUL
THROUGH MODERN ETHERIC MOVEMENT

Robert Powell

The human being is an expression of the ever-unfolding wisdom of the creative Logos, the Word. The whole of creation bears the imprint of the cosmic sounding. This book describes a way, through movement and gesture, to work with the creative, sounding principle that manifests in the Earth's enveloping life sphere. Today, the increasingly binding and hardening conditions of modern life now threatens the divine seed of life here on Earth, which has been fructified and developed over the millennia. Creation—coming to expression through the flowering of the cosmic breath—is losing its natural connection with humanity and with Mother Earth, which are increasingly given over to anti-life forces, comprising destruction, inversions, and lifeless replicas of creation's gifts.

The sacred movements described in this book arise from the modern art of movement known as *eurythmy* (Greek: "good movement"), which came into the world in 1912. These sacred gestures, when practiced with the words gifted to humanity by the incarnated Logos two thousand years ago, lead us back to our connection with the fullness of creation and toward the goal of developing the body of immortality, the resurrection body. In 2012, we celebrated the one-hundredth anniversary of the birth of eurythmy. This book invites us to partake of the richness of the sacred through life-enhancing movement and gesture as a path to reconnect with the cosmic formative forces that sound the call of resurrection.

The wealth of material included in this book educates the soul toward awaking to a conscious understanding of humanity's divine heritage and true calling. The exercises in this work provide a training that ennobles and refines the qualities of the human soul.

ISBN: 9781584201175 I 240 pages I pbk I $25.00

Astrogeographia

Correspondences between the Stars and Earthly Locations
A Bible of Astrology and Earth Chakras

Robert Powell and David Bowden

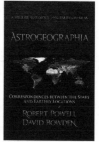

"As above, so below" is the foundation of all star wisdom. It was known in ancient times that there are correspondences between the macrocosm (heavenly realm) and the microcosm (human being) and the Earth. Astrogeographia is a modern form of that ancient star wisdom. According to the astronomer Johannes Kepler:

> "There radiates into the Earth soul an image of the sense-perceptible zodiac and the whole firmament as a bond of sympathy between Heaven and Earth.... This imprint into the Earth soul through the sense-perceptible zodiac and the entire sphere of fixed stars is also confirmed through observation."

Moreover, Rudolf Steiner said in his course on astronomy, "We can conceive of the active heavenly sphere mirrored in the Earth." The authors of *Astrogeographia* set out to determine the correspondences between the starry heavens and the earthly globe: *As above, so below.*

There are numerous books on the sacredness and the spirituality of our Earth. However, few books deal with the relationship between the Earth and the cosmos, which is the central theme for the research presented in *Astrogeographia*. Its point of departure is the one-to-one correspondence between the encircling starry heavens—the celestial sphere—and the sphere of the earthly globe. David Bowden has not only worked out the mathematics of this one-to-one correspondence, but has also written a computer program that applies it in practice. Thus, a new science has been born—Astrogeographia—concerning the one-to-one correspondence between the earthly sphere and the celestial sphere.

ISBN: 9781584201335 | 360 pages | pbk | $25.00

THE SOPHIA FOUNDATION was founded and exists to help usher in the new Age of Sophia and the corresponding Sophianic culture, the Rose of the World, prophesied by Daniel Andreev and other spiritual teachers. Part of the work of the Sophia Foundation is the cultivation of a new star wisdom, *Astro-Sophia* (Astrosophy), now arising in our time in response to the descent of Sophia, who is the bearer of Divine Wisdom, just as Christ (the Logos, or the Lamb) is the bearer of Divine Love. Like the star wisdom of antiquity, Astrosophy is sidereal, which means "of the stars." Astrosophy, inspired by Divine Sophia, descending from stellar heights, directs our consciousness toward the glory and majesty of the starry heavens, to encompass the entire celestial sphere of our cosmos and, beyond this, to the galactic realm—the realm that Daniel Andreev referred to as "the heights of our universe"—from which Sophia is descending on her path of approach into our cosmos. Sophia draws our attention not only to the star mysteries of the heights, but also to the cosmic mysteries connected with Christ's deeds of redemption wrought two thousand years ago. To penetrate these mysteries is the purpose of the yearly *Journal for Star Wisdom*.

For information about Astrosophy/Choreocosmos/
Cosmic Dance workshops
Contact the Sophia Foundation:
4500 19th Street, #369, Boulder, CO 80304
Phone: (303) 242-5388
sophia@sophiafoundation.org
www.sophiafoundation.org

ROBERT POWELL has an enduring passion for the stars, and was awarded a PhD for his contribution to the History of the Zodiac. He is an internationally renowned lecturer. Through the content of his talks at conferences and workshops, his living knowledge of the stars is woven into his presentations. As well as being a scholar of the history of astronomy, Robert is also a movement therapist trained in the art of eurythmy (from the Greek meaning beautiful, harmonious movement). Focusing upon the cosmic aspects of eurythmy he founded the Choreocosmos School of Cosmic and Sacred Dance, and he leads cosmic dances (dancing with the stars) in endeavoring to create harmony between the heavens, the Earth, humanity, and nature. He presents Choreocosmos workshops in various parts of the world, including Europe and Australia. Robert is also cofounder of the Sophia Foundation and the Sophia Grail Circle, through which he facilitates sacred celebrations dedicated to the Divine Feminine. With Karen Rivers, cofounder of the Sophia Foundation, he leads pilgrimages to the world's sacred sites: Turkey, 1996; the Holy Land, 1997; France, 1998; Britain, 2000; Italy, 2002; Greece, 2004; Egypt, 2006; India, 2008; Turkey, 2009; the Grand Canyon, 2010; South Africa, 2012; and Peru, 2014.

Robert is the author of many books, including *The Astrological Revolution* and *Christ and the Maya Calendar* (both coauthored by Kevin Dann); *The Mystery, Biography & Destiny of Mary Magdalene* and *Prophecy–Phenomena–Hope: The Real Meaning of 2012*. Robert is also editor of the yearly *Journal for Star Wisdom*. He also wrote two books with Lacquanna Paul: *Cosmic Dances of the Zodiac* and *Cosmic Dances of the Planets*, which not only describe cosmic dance but also contain a wealth of research material. For texts relating to sacred dance, see *The Prayer Sequence in Sacred Dance* and *The Foundation Stone Meditation in the Sacred Dance of Eurythmy* (both written with Lacquanna Paul). Robert's most recent books are *Astrogeographia: Correspondences between the Stars and Earthly Locations* (coauthored by David Bowden) and *Gautama Buddha's Successor: A Force for Good in Our Time* (coauthored with Estelle Isaacson). For further information on his books and courses, visit:

www.sophiafoundation.org or www.astrogeographia.org
or steinerbooks.org/books/AuthorDetail.aspx?id=23981

ESTELLE ISAACSON is a contemporary mystic and seer whose first two books were published by LogoSophia in 2012: *Through the Eyes of Mary Magdalene: Early Years and Soul Awakening.* In this first book in a trilogy on the life of Mary Magdalene, Estelle Isaacson presents her visions of the life of Christ as seen through Magdalene's own eyes. The second book, *Through the Eyes of Mary*  *Magdalene: From Initiation to the Passion,* enters the profound mysteries of Christ's Passion, culminating in the Resurrection. Estelle Isaacson is coauthor with Robert Powell of *Gautama Buddha's Successor: A Force for Good in Our Time* (2013).